REACHING
FOR THE SKY

ONE HUNDRED DEFINING MOMENTS
FROM THE ROYAL AIR FORCE 1918-2018

REACHING
FOR THE SKY

ONE HUNDRED DEFINING MOMENTS
FROM THE ROYAL AIR FORCE 1918-2018

SCOTT ADDINGTON

UNIFORM

FOR ALL THOSE
MAGNIFICENT MEN AND WOMEN
AND THEIR FLYING MACHINES

Contents

Introduction

The Royal Air Force is much more than just the flying part of the British armed forces – it is an institution; a national treasure; something of which all British people should be rightly proud. The RAF has been at the forefront of aviation innovation since its inception in 1918 and during the subsequent one hundred years has enjoyed many hundreds of defining moments that has made compiling a list of just one hundred for this book quite an impossible task. There has simply been too many to choose from!

There were a number of ways I could have gone about the business of deciding which moments to include here. I could have sorted them all in alphabetical order and picked the top 100, I could have performed my own 'lottery draw' by giving each one a number and picking the first 100 out of a hat; or I could have got my kids to choose them for me. None of these options seemed like they would do the job justice though, so instead I decided to work on a mix of moments that showcased the best of the RAF (and earlier organisations such as the Royal Flying Corps and Royal Naval Air Service) across a number of different areas, including its organisation, the use of technology, its undoubted courage, inspirational personalities and of course some of the most iconic aircraft in the history of aviation.

The result is a very subjective and personal list of defining moments. I accept and acknowledge that some readers may disagree with my list, but I hope that the stories, machines and technologies that I have included strike a chord with the reader.

Scott Addington

Timeline

1 April 1918

Formation of the Royal Air Force

21 April 1918

The Red Baron shot down

3 June 1918

The DFC, AFC, DFM and AFM are all instituted

6 June 1918

The Independent Air Force – the RAF's strategic bombing arm, is formed

1 April 1924

The Fleet Air Arm was formed

27 January 1921

The RAF Nursing Service (RAFNS) was formed

3 July 1920

The first RAF Pageant took place at Hendon – with 60,000 spectators

1 April 1920

RAF Central Band is formed at Uxbridge

1 May 1924

The RAF's first all metal fighter plane – the Armstrong Whitworth Siskin III – enters service

9 March – 1 May 1925

RAF's first independent air action at Waziristan, India

29 October 1925

The Observer Corps formed

23 December 1928

The world's first airlift is carried out by the RAF in the Kabul Airlift

● **World War 1**

● **World War 2**

29 November 1939

RAuxAF Spitfires shoot down a Heinkel He111 bomber over Scotland. The first German plane to be shot down over the UK in WW2

5 September 1939

First RAF attack on an enemy U-Boat

28 June 1939

Creation of the Women's Auxiliary Air Force (WAAF)

16 May 1940

Air Chief Marshall Sir Hugh Dowding writes to the Air Ministry to stop them sending more fighter squadrons to France

11 March 1940

First U-Boat sunk by the RAF

14 October 1918

Dropping of the 1,650lb 'SN' bomb – the largest bomb of WW1

11 January 1919

Dept of Civil Aviation was created by Air Ministry

24 March 1919

First group of WRAFs (the Ladies of the Rhine) arrived in France

14/15 June 1919

RAF officers Capt J. Alcock & Lt A. Whitten-Brown make first non-stop flight across the Atlantic Ocean in 16 hrs 27 mins

1 January 1920

RAF Apprentice Scheme began

23 October 1919

RAF Benevolent Fund founded by Lord Trenchard

6 July 1919

Airship R34 completes first airship crossing of Atlantic

26 October 1931

First flight of classic trainer aircraft, the de Havilland Tiger Moth

5 March 1936

Prototype of Supermarine Spitfire flew for the first time

1 July 1936

Approval given to formation of the Royal Air Force Volunteer Reserve

14 July 1936

RAF organised into four commands: Bomber, Fighter Coastal and Training

1 November 1938

RAF Balloon Command formed to control all UK based barrage balloon units

1 April 1938

Maintenance Command formed

24 April 1940

The Air Council establishes a Technical Branch within the RAF

4 June 1940

RAF takes part in Operation Dynamo over the beaches of Dunkirk

10 June – 31 October 1940

Battle of Britain

1 February 1941

The Air Training Corps was introduced

Timeline (continued)

15 May 1941

Maiden flight of the first British jet plane – The Gloster E.28/39

24 December 1941

The Avro Lancaster enters service with the RAF

30 May 1942

Thousand bomber raid over Cologne

1 June 1942

Thousand bomber raid over Essen

6 July 1949

Two Spitfires of No. 60 Squadron fly first offensive mission against Malayan terrorists

28 June 1948 – 30 September 1949

Operation Plainfare – The Berlin Airlift over Cologne

1 February 1949

Women's Auxiliary Air Force (WAAF) renamed Women's Royal Air Force (WRAF)

1 May 1950

The first British Operational Helicopter Unit, the Far East Air Force's Casualty Evacuation Flight, was established

20 September 1950

Plt Officer Jean Lennox Bird became the first woman to be awarded RAF Pilot's Wings

13 February 1954

The first British Swept-Wing fighter – the Supermarine Swift – enters service

4 November 1976

The British Aerospace Hawk enters service

1 April 1969

The world's first vertical take-off and landing aircraft – the Hawker-Siddeley Harrier – entered service with No. 233 OCU, RAF Wittering

30 April 1968

RAF Bomber and Fighter Commands merge to create RAF Strike Command

30 April 1982

Operation Black Buck – Vulcan bombers take off on the first of six raids against Argentinian positions in the Falklands

16 January – 11 April 1991

RAF aircraft take part in the air battle over Kuwait and Iraq in the Gulf War

16-19 December 1998

Tornado GR1s fly 250 missions against targets in Operation Desert Fox

25 June 1942

Thousand bomber raid over Bremen

30 January 1943

Daylight raid on Berlin on the 10th anniversary of the Nazi regime

16-17 May 1943

Operations Chastise – Dambusters Raid

6 June 1944

Operation Overlord – D-Day

7 November 1945

A Meteor IV piloted by Group Capt H. J. Wilson achieves speed record for jet powered aircraft of 606.25 mph

15 May 1945

A Gloster Pioneer makes RAF's first jet-powered flight

17–25 September 1944

Operation Market Garden

1 April 1954

The final operation flight made by a Spitfire. A reconnaissance flight during Operation Firedog in Malaya

1 June 1956

No. 216 Sqn at Lyneham became the first jet transportation squadron in the world using the de Havilland Comet

15 May 1965

First official public display of The Red Arrows at the Biggin Hill International Air Fair

15 May 1959

Last operational flight made by an RAF Flying Boat (Sunderland)

11 July 1957

Historic Aircraft Flight is formed at Biggin Hill with 1 Hurricane and 3 Spitfires

31 October 1956

RAF Canberra fly reconnaissance sorties and bomb Egyptian airfields during the Suez crisis

30 October – 31 December 2004

Four Tornado F3s deployed as part of NATO's Baltic Air Policing mission

11 December 2009

The Atlas (A400M) prototype made its first flight

19 July 2012

RAF receives its first F-35B Lightning stealth combat aircraft

4 October 2015

The RAF's Search and Rescue fleet are retired

Organisational
Moments

01 Early Foundations – Military Balloons

It is not too far fetched to state that British military aeronautics began its journey with the Royal Engineers. In 1862, Lieutenant Edward Grover approached the War Office with the idea that the use of balloons should be seriously considered as a tool for military observation and reconnaissance. The War Office were not convinced but did allow Grover to conduct some low-level trials at Aldershot, although it wasn't until 1878 that official trials commenced at the newly opened Balloon Equipment Store located at Woolwich.

One of the officers stationed at the new Balloon Equipment Store was a Captain James Templar; a member of the Middlesex Militia and a keen amateur balloonist. He already owned a coal-gas balloon named *Crusader* – the first vessel of its type to be used by the army – and soon got to work on a new design. *Pioneer* was a 10,000cu.ft hydrogen balloon, specially constructed from varnished cambric for £71. Pioneer took to the skies on 23 August 1878.

And so was born the British air arm.

When the Boer War broke out in October 1899 the British Army only had a single balloon section and depot stationed at Aldershot. Nonetheless, an aerial section of Royal Engineers was sent out to South Africa and, despite a less than auspicious

start where aerial observations made before the Battle of Magersfontein were largely ignored resulting in heavy infantry losses, the reputation of the balloon section gathered rapid momentum. Despite only being able to be used in good weather and inflation times of up to ten hours, positive results during the Siege of Ladysmith and the advance on Pretoria saw the size of the balloon detachment increased to twenty-one NCOs and men. As the nineteenth century gave way to the twentieth, technical innovations such as the transmission and receipt of wireless communications were worked on. Handling and control of unpowered balloons was also improved, which would become invaluable in WW1 as huge numbers of observation and barrage balloons would be required.

◀ **Royal Engineers observation balloon c1900**

£150

the amount of money the War Office allocated to the newly opened Balloon Equipment Store in 1878 for maintenance and equipment.

Balloon Equipment Store (Woolwich 1878)

Balloon School and Factory (Chatham 1882)

Balloon Section - Royal Engineers (1890)

Air Battalion - Royal Engineers (1911)

No 1 Company (Lighter than Air) Royal Engineers

Royal Flying Corps Military Wing (1912)

No 2 Company (Heavier than Air) Royal Engineers

02 **Man Lifting Kites**

Although balloons had many supporters in the upper echelons of the British Army, their limitations in deployment (due to weather and the time it took to get them airborne) forced them to investigate viable alternatives.

Experiments with kites started back in 1893 and in 1894 Major B. F. S. Baden-Powell of the Scots Guards had succeeded in putting together a group of kites capable of lifting a man 100ft in the air. As a result of these early trials, a kite section was formed within the Royal Engineers that same year. However, it was a kite designed by a brash American named Samuel Franklin Cody that would eventually be accepted by the War Office. Cody approached the War Office initially in 1901 but was quickly dismissed, however the Admiralty were interested enough to run a trial that saw Cody flying 800 feet above the rear of *HMS Seahorse*. All was going fine until the ship turned down wind, the kite collapsed and Cody had to be rescued from the sea. Despite this calamity, the Admiralty placed an order for kites.

Cody's kites consisted of a pilot kite below which were three to seven lifting kites (depending on the strength of the wind), suspended beneath these was a carrier kite, below which was the observer's basket. This system was capable of lifting an observer up to an altitude of 1,500ft.

After crossing the English Channel in November 1903 in a small boat drawn by kites, Cody re-visited the War Office in 1904. Following successful demonstrations in winds of 40mph the War Office were completely ecstatic. They ordered three kites and appointed Cody as Chief Instructor of Kiting.

Despite never being used operationally, kites remained in use with both the navy and army up until the beginning of WW1. The Army List of August 1914 includes a Kite Section of the RFC stationed at South Farnborough.

Kite Communications

Cody proposed to the War Office that in a military situation the passenger be equipped with a telescope, telephone, camera and gun. If the telephone did not function correctly messages could be blown up the cable and returned by the passenger in weighted bags. These would simply slide down the cable.

"I cannot speak too strongly as to the excellence of these kites as regards their design and ability to perform what Mr Cody claims for them. The man-lifting kites will take a man into the air to practically any required height and will keep him steady there so that he can observe. No other kites that I have read or heard of can approach them in sturdiness and security combined with lifting power."

Colonel John E. Capper, Commanding Officer, Balloon Section, Royal Engineers

03 Airships

With the advent of the internal combustion engine it didn't take long before people were wondering how to utilise engines to enable some kind of powered flight. In early 1902, James Templer, an officer in the Balloon Section of the Royal Engineers, gained consent from the War Office to conduct research into non-rigid airships. Two years later construction began on British Army Dirigible No. 1, better known as *Nulli Secundus* (Latin for 'Second to None') – Britain's first powered military aircraft – but it wouldn't be ready to fly until 1907, a full seven years after the Germans had launched their first Zeppelin. While the 55,000 cubic feet *Nulli Secundus* was struggling to get to grips with a round trip from Farnborough to London, the German's were flying Zeppelins that were almost ten times the size of the British example, several hundred miles.

Britain was way behind in terms of airship construction and technology.

Nulli Secundus was rebuilt as *Nulli Secundus II* and enjoyed an increase in gas capacity from 55,000 to 85,000 cubic feet and was launched on 24 July 1908. However, it was broken up within a year.

A smaller airship was then constructed and named *Baby*. It took its maiden flight in 1909 but soon developed engine stability trouble and was rebuilt,

expanded and renamed *Beta*. *Beta* would prove to be slightly more successful than both versions of *Nulli Secundus* and was used in many army manoeuvres including the testing of wireless communications.

Meanwhile, the Royal Navy were also interested in airships to work as aerial scouts for their fleets when out at sea. *The Mayfly* was 66ft (20m) longer than the most recent Zeppelin and held fifty per cent more gas, however on 24 September 1911, as it was being moved out of its shed prior to testing, it broke its back and never actually flew.

The army built three more airships, but shortly after the last one was completed in August 1913 the Royal Navy was given control of airship development and No. 1 Squadron RFC (formally No. 1 Company Airships) was transferred over to the navy. Thus ended the short and not very successful era of airships in the army.

The Gamma Airship

Nulli Secundus

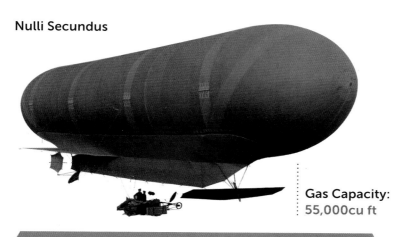

Gas Capacity:
55,000cu ft

Length: **120ft (36.59m)**

Crew:

3 👤👤👤

Max Speed:
40
mph
(64 km/h)

Power:
50
hp

Ox Skin

The 'envelope' of the airship was made of goldbeaters skin (produced from the gut of an ox) which was not only exceptionally strong and flexible but also very light. The average size of each piece of skin used was approximately 24 inches long and 10 inches wide and twelve layers were needed to reach the required strength.

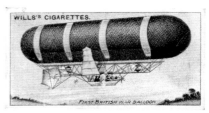

Cigarette card featuring Nulli Secundus

World History Archive / Alamy

04 The Royal Flying Corps

Recommendations for the formation of a flying corps was accepted on 13 April 1912 – establishing the Royal Flying Corps, which initially consisted of a naval wing, an army wing as well as a flying school. Initial strength was 133 officers and by the end of 1912 it could boast twelve manned balloons and thirty-six aircraft.

However, it quickly became obvious that the Royal Navy had different ideas and priorities for its air division. On 1 July 1914, the naval arm separated to form the Royal Naval Air Service, leaving the Royal Flying Corps to continue as the official air arm of the British Army.

On 13 August 1914, sixty machines from 2, 3 and 4 Squadrons RFC departed from Dover to join up with the British Expeditionary Force in France. Six days later they took part in their first action of WW1 with two machines taking part in a reconnaissance patrol.

One of the most important roles of the RFC during the war was observing artillery fire above enemy targets that could not be seen by spotters on the ground. Initially the only way a pilot could communicate with an artillery battery was to drop handwritten reports back to the battery until wireless telegraphy was introduced in late 1914, although in those early days it was far from reliable. Aerial photography was another area in which the RFC was employed and by 1916 the art of photo-reconnaisance was quite advanced, so much so, that the entire Somme offensive in the summer of 1916 was based on the RFC's photography.

As the war rumbled on the RFC became more and more involved in ground attacks in an effort to disrupt enemy forces at or near the front line. While tactical bombing raids (sometimes using home-made bombs thrown out of the cockpit) were often planned and aimed at specific targets, ground attacks were commonly carried out by individual pilots in the heat of battle. Often these ground attacks could cause significant damage to the enemy but they were not without danger as any direct hit from ground fire could bring an aircraft down.

During 1917 the RFC started to suffer at the hands of the German Air Force who had quality pilots and superior fighters. This superiority culminated in 'Bloody April' which saw the RFC suffer very heavy losses indeed while supporting army operations during the Battle of Arras.

In order to more effectively organise Britain's air services it was decided to merge the Royal Flying Corps and the Royal Naval Air Service to create a brand new, independent air service: the Royal Air Force.

SE5 A8907, equipped with a Lewis Gun and piloted by the British Ace, Captain Albert Ball who served the No. 56 Squadron RAF

Founded: April 1912

Motto: *Per Ardua ad Astra* (Through Adversity to the Stars)

Size (March 1918): 144,078 (incl 18,286 officers)

Disbanded: Merged into the Royal Air Force 1 April 1918

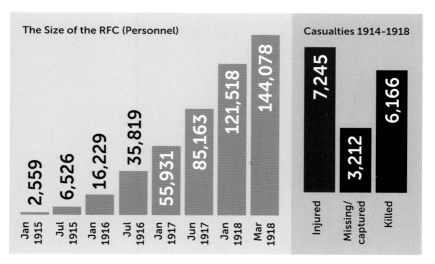

The Size of the RFC (Personnel)

2,559	6,526	16,229	35,819	55,931	85,163	121,518	144,078
Jan 1915	Jul 1915	Jan 1916	Jul 1916	Jan 1917	Jun 1917	Jan 1918	Mar 1918

Casualties 1914-1918

Injured	Missing/ captured	Killed
7,245	3,212	6,166

"I wish particularly to bring to your Lordships' notice the admirable work done by the Royal Flying Corps under Sir David Henderson. Their skill, energy, and perseverance has been beyond all praise. They have furnished me with most complete and accurate information, which has been of incalculable value in the conduct of operations. Fired at constantly by friend and foe, and not hesitating to fly in every kind of weather, they have remained undaunted throughout. Further, by actually fighting in the air, they have succeeded in destroying five of the enemy's machines."

Official dispatch from Sir John French. 7 September 1914

05 Netheravon Concentration Camp

In the summer of 1914, the commander of the military wing of the Royal Flying Corps, Colonel Frederick Sykes, ordered all his squadrons to converge at Netheravon Airfield Camp (on Salisbury Plain) for training, planning and to practise mobilisation.

This 'call to arms' affected just four full squadrons – a total of around 60 aircraft, 700 officers and men along with approximately 150 support vehicles – but despite this relatively small number of men and machines getting everyone to Netheravon wasn't easy. No. 2 Squadron were based in Scotland, some 570 miles from Netheravon and many of their vehicles could only travel at a top speed of 10mph! Not surprisingly, it took No. 2 Squadron two weeks to get there.

Once everyone had eventually arrived at camp the group experimented with methods of observation, reconnaissance, photography and flying training. It wasn't all work though, Wednesday and Saturday afternoons were given over to sports and recreation.

The camp began to break up in early July 1914 with the shadow of war looming large on the horizon. No. 2 Squadron started their long and slow trek back north – finally getting back home on 19 July. In retrospect, the timing of this camp was perfect as just over a month after the camp ended, Britain declared war on Germany. Very soon after that those chaps who had practised and honed their skills at Netheravon during the summer of 1914 would have the opportunity to show the world what they had learnt.

During the war, Netheravon was one of the main training bases for would-be pilots and even continued to help train pilots after the war had finished, becoming the home of No. 1 Flying Training School. With the outbreak of WW2 Netheravon was used by various squadrons and in the run up to the Normandy Invasion became the main training centre for Glider Squadrons and Paratroopers.

After the war, RAF flying operations at Netheravon slowly declined and in the 1950s it became a training centre for the RAF Police. In 1963, the site was transferred over to the Army Air Corps and in subsequent years was used by various units including the Territorial Army and the Brigade of Gurkhas.

Today, the airfield is used by the Joint Services Parachute Centre, part of the army's programme for serving and injured personnel, and is home to the Army Parachute Association, a charity which supports sports parachuting for serving and retired personnel.

**RFC aircraft and tents at
Netheravon, June 1914**

Netheravon,
Salisbury Plain

06 The Royal Naval Air Service

Although the Royal Naval Air Service was not formally established until July 1914 the Admiralty had been playing around with kites and balloons, primarily for at sea reconnaissance, from as early as 1903 and by 1908 the government was actively looking at options for official use of aircraft for naval purposes. In November 1910, the Royal Aero Club granted the Royal Navy two machines and some instructors to help train pilots. They also offered the use of an airfield at Eastchurch on the Isle of Sheppey. Not surprisingly the navy accepted!

Meanwhile, the government were still debating and discussing how to organise an air defence and on 13 April 1912 the Royal Flying Corps was constituted by Royal Warrant. It took over control of the tiny navy air detachment as well as the Air Battalion of the Royal Engineers. The first couple of years as the naval wing of the RFC saw a period of rapid expansion and technological advances; the first flight from a moving ship, the first seaplane carrier was commissioned and a series of coastal air stations were built to aid air/sea operations. Tensions were beginning to run high with many people in the Admiralty pushing hard for the navy to have their own air wing that they could run independently of the army. Their wish was eventually granted on 1 July 1914 when the naval wing of the Royal Flying Corps was renamed the Royal Naval Air Service. The strength

of this new service at its inception was ninety-three aircraft, six airships, two balloons and 727 personnel, but most importantly, all aircraft and personnel were now administered and controlled by the navy.

The main roles of the RNAS were naval fleet reconnaissance, attacking enemy coastal areas and defending Britain from enemy attack. The RNAS also operated fighter squadrons on the Western Front. By the outbreak of war in August 1914 the RNAS had more aircraft under its control than the RFC. Rivalry with the RFC was intense, yet it tended to be the RFC pilots such as Albert Ball and James McCudden who attracted the limelight and publicity rather than the RNAS pilots, despite some daring raids against the enemy. On Christmas Day 1914, the RNAS attacked German Zeppelin bases at Cuxhaven and Wilhelmshaven. During the Gallipoli campaign an RNAS pilot, Flight Commander C. Edmonds, attacked a Turkish ship with a torpedo slung underneath his aircraft. Edwards attacked flying in just fifteen feet above the sea and managed to sink his target.

On 1 April 1918, the RNAS was merged with the RFC to form the new Royal Air Force. At the time of the merger the RNAS boasted 55,000 personnel, 2,949 aircraft and 103 airships.

Founded: 1 July 1914

Headquarters: Eastchurch

Disbanded: 1 April 1918

Naval Air First

On 10 January 1912 Commander C Samson took off from HMS *Hibernia* in a modified hydro-plane to be the first pilot to take off from a ship at sea.

RNAS Ace

The leading RNAS air 'Ace' of the First World War was Canadian born pilot Raymond Collishaw CB, OBE, DSO & Bar, DSC, DFC with sixty recorded victories.

RNAS Short Type 184

	Personnel	Aircraft	Airships
1914	727	93	6
1918	55,000	2,949	103

"12th: Got up at 2.45am. Edmonds on a new Sunbeam Short and myself on my old machine were hoisted out at 4.30, after two or three things being done on my machine which were found necessary at the last moment. Edmonds rose well with his torpedo, but I took twenty minutes trying to persuade my old bus to lift. After twenty minutes, by violent piloting and determination I got off, which gave me much delight. However, my delight was short lived for after ten minutes the engine spluttered out and I had to land. After a quick look around nothing seemed wrong, so I made another attempt and after twelve minutes the same thing happened, so just as Edmonds was returning I was obliged to give it up. I was bitterly disappointed not to have been able to be the first to actually torpedo an enemy ship."

Flight Lieutenant George Bentley Dacre DSO, RNAS

07 April 1918 – The creation of the world's first independent air force

In broad daylight on 25 May 1917, a squadron of German Gotha bombers made their first bombing raid on England, attacking the Kent port of Folkestone, killing ninety-five people. The public reaction to these bombings was outrage, anger and panic, and when another raid hit a London school on 12 June killing eighteen children, this outrage was turned up several notches. Something had to be done.

A London Air Defence area was quickly set up with large numbers of anti-aircraft guns, searchlights and aircraft made available. At the same time a South African military leader, General Jan Smuts, was asked by the War Cabinet to consider workable solutions. His final report, now known as the *Smuts Report*, recommended that Britain's air service should be treated as a separate force, away from the commands of the navy and the army. Instead a new force should be created that would be solely responsible for conducting warfare in the air.

Following the report, Parliament debated and passed the Air Force (Constitution) Act 1917, which was given Royal Assent by King George V on the 29 November 1917. A few months later, on 1 April 1918, the Royal Naval Air Service and the Royal Flying Corps were merged together to create something new, despite opposition from senior figures in both the British Army and Royal Navy. The Royal Air Force was formed as a separate service, independent of both army and navy – the first time any country had a completely autonomous and independent air force. The new service even had its own ministry under Lord Rothermere, the first Secretary of State for Air.

Not only was the Royal Air Force the only independent air force in the world, it was also the most powerful with over 22,000 aircraft and over 300,000 personnel.

Founded: 1 April 1918

Motto: *Per Ardua ad Astra* (Through Adversity to the Stars)

Headquarters: RAF High Wycombe

Strength on 1 April 1918: c22,000 aircraft, c300,000 personnel

"There is absolutely no limit to the scale of its future independent war use."

General Jan Christian Smuts

08 No 1 Squadron RAF – First In All Things

No. 1 Squadron, RAF was the first operational squadron in service after the formation of the Royal Air Force on 1 April 1918. Not surprisingly, its motto is *In Omnibus Princeps* (First in all Things).

The origins of the squadron can be traced all the way back to 1878 with the formation of the No. 1 Balloon Company which eventually turned into the Air Battalion of the Royal Engineers on 1 April 1911.

Now part of No. 1 Group, RAF, the squadron is based at RAF Lossiemouth where it carries out its role as a multi-purpose combat squadron equipped with a fleet of Eurofighter Typhoon FGR4s.

Pilots, officers and men of No1 Squadron, RAF stand among their SE5 machines. This picture was taken at Clairmarais, France in July 1918, just three months after the birth of the RAF

Formation: 1 April 1911 (Royal Engineers) 13 May 1912 (Royal Flying Corps) 1 April 1918 (Royal Air Force)

Home Station: RAF Lossiemouth

Motto: *In omnibus princeps* (First in all things)

Current aircraft: Eurofighter Typhoon FGR4

09 Women's Royal Air Force

During WW1 thousands of women from the Women's Royal Naval Service (WRNS) and the Women's Army Auxiliary Corps (WAAC) did invaluable work in and around the airfields and bases of the Royal Flying Corps and Royal Naval Air Service.

With the proposed merger of the RFC and RNAS there were concerns raised about the potential loss of this specialised female workforce – this led the powers that be to form the Women's Royal Air Force (WRAF) on the very same day the RAF was born.

Those ladies already serving in the WAAC and WRNS were given the opportunity to join the WRAF and 9,000 women made the switch to the new outfit. The numbers of the WRAF were further boosted by the enrolment of civilians. The minimum age for female volunteers was eighteen and included quite a stringent health check. Educated women, or those from a wealthy family, were generally enrolled as officers whilst the rest (the majority) were recruited as 'members'. These members were classed as either mobile (could be placed anywhere at short notice) or immobile (were formally attached to their local station or base).

Originally the plan for the WRAF was to provide female mechanics so the men could concentrate on combat roles, but so many women enrolled that the service was quickly expanded to cover many varied positions such as technical fitters, admin clerks, welders, photography, driving and tailoring. Despite a rocky beginning the WRAF soon won over many of its male counterparts in the RAF and was widely respected and looked upon as an invaluable asset to the RAF. However, it was formed during a time of war and, with the RAF facing cutbacks in the post war era, the WRAF was disbanded in 1920. By this time the WRAF was 32,000 strong.

The WRAF was reborn on 1 February 1949, offering women a full-time career in the air force for the first time. Right from the outset it was planned that the WRAF was to be as integrated as possible with the RAF and almost straight away eighty per cent of trades were open to women. The only real restriction was they could not undertake combatant duties. Over the coming years both the WRAF and RAF grew ever closer and in 1968 female officers adopted the rank titles of their RAF counterparts. Training was also consolidated both at recruit and officer level, and in 1970 the first female entrants were admitted into the RAF College, Cranwell.

On 1 April 1994, the WRAF formally merged with the RAF. In forty-five years women had progressed from a temporary wartime support role to become full members of the world's oldest independent air force.

WRAF recruitment
poster – 1918

Founded: 1 April 1918

Disbanded: 1920

Strength in 1920: 32,000

Re-instituted: 1 Feb 1949

**Merged with RAF
1 April 1994**

IWM Q 27562

WRAF working on a De Havilland 9A

First operational female pilot

Julie Ann Gibson was the first female pilot
for the Royal Air Force when she graduated
on 14 June 1991 at No. 6 Flying Training
School RAF. She was assigned to No. 32
Squadron RAF, where she flew Hawker
Siddeley Andovers before being promoted
to Flight Lieutenant and assigned to fly
Lockheed C-130 Hercules at RAF Lyneham.

Michael Powell / Alamy

Kirsty Moore, the first ever
female pilot with the RAF
display team the Red Arrows

31

10 ATA – Air Transport Auxiliary

WW1 had transformed aircraft production into a booming industry in Britain and during the 1920s and 1930s with flying clubs popping up all over the country. In 1938, and war with Germany almost inevitable, a young British Airways director called Gerard d'Erlanger approached the government to discuss the possibility for pilots who were not eligible to join the RAF or Fleet Air Arm to help out in case of war. The government listened to his ideas and in 1939 he set out his plans for a force of civil pilots to fly light aircraft carrying supplies, casualties, messages etc.

Within days of war breaking out, female pilot Pauline Gower met with the ATA to discuss the idea of her joining up. The RAF had been very resistant to the idea of female pilots but she was sure that she, and many female pilots like her, could substantially help the war effort. In December 1939, she was appointed leader of a new women's section of the ATA. In January 1940, the first eight female pilots were unveiled at a press launch; eventually 166 women would fly with the ATA.

Initially there was very little work given to the pilots of the ATA perhaps due to a lack of trust from their RAF colleagues, but they quickly proved themselves and by May 1940 the ATA had taken over the transportation of all military aircraft from factories to maintenance units and by August that year they were responsible for all aircraft ferrying roles, freeing up thousands of RAF combat pilots for active duty.

The first ATA pilots were trained at the RAF's Central Flying School but the ATA soon developed their own training regime which saw pilots start off with single-engine light aircraft before moving up to more powerful and complex machines in stages. Those qualified in one 'class' of aircraft then gained experience through viable ferrying work with any and all aircraft in that class before taking on new training for the next class. A pilot cleared to work on one or more classes of aircraft could be called upon to ferry any kind of aircraft on which he or she was qualified, so a pilot who was trained in moving big four-engine bombers could quite as easily be called up to move a small single-engine light aircraft if that was needed at the time.

As the war drew to a close, the demand for the ferrying services of the ATA decreased and eventually stopped altogether. After VE Day, ATA pilots started to return to their civilian occupations and their bases were closed. The ATA was formally closed on 30 November 1945 after providing a vital war flying service.

1318 pilots

2786 ground staff

151 flight engineers

They delivered more than **309,000** aircraft

During the war the ATA flew **415,000** hours

About **883** tonnes of freight carried

3430 passengers transported

Founded: 1939

Motto: *Aetheris Avidi* (Eager for the Air)

Headquarters: White Waltham, Maidenhead

Disbanded: 30 November 1945

Attagirls

One thing that set the ATA apart was that they accepted female pilots. Nicknamed Attagirls, 168 female pilots served with the ATA. Fifteen of these women would lose their lives, including First Officer Amy Johnson CBE, legendary English female aviator and the first woman to fly solo from Britain to Australia, who died while serving with the ATA in 1941

174 ATA pilots were killed

Ancient and Tattered

The ATA recruited pilots who were considered to be unsuitable for either the Royal Air Force or the Fleet Air Arm by reason of age, fitness or gender. As a result the ATA was often referred to as "Ancient and Tattered Airmen".

"We used to get very tired. One night, I fell asleep in my Spitfire. I don't know for how long but when I woke up I was still flying straight and level. Later that night, I went to a party with an air force bloke and when we arrived I put my head on his shoulder and I woke up at six o'clock. 'That was a lovely party,' he said and brought me home again."

Marie Agazarian, Female pilot with the Air Transport Auxilliary

11 Royal Auxiliary Air Force

Lord Trenchard wanted the RAF to be supplemented with a reserve of trained personnel, capable of stepping up to regular service during times of conflict. His vision became reality in October 1924 with the first Auxiliary Air Force (AAF) squadrons starting to form in early 1925.

In those days the AAF squadrons tended to form at a town or city level, and were mostly centred around a local aerodrome. Recruits tended to be local along similar lines to the Territorial Army, but as AAF members were expected to obtain their own pilot licenses at a cost of £96 (approximately £5,000 today) the members of the AAF tended to be rather more well-healed than the average TA member. Pilot members of the AAF were required to sign up for a minimum of five years, fly a certain number of hours per year, and attend a fifteen-day training camp each year.

As war loomed once more the RAF Volunteer Reserve (RAFVR) was formed to supplement the AAF and provide more men in case of war. The RAFVR tended to be former members of the RAF who had left the service or pilots from flying schools. Any AAF member whose five-year engagement expired and who wanted to continue to serve was then asked to join the RAFVR.

By the time war did eventually break out there were more than 100,000 men in the RAFVR, an additional twenty auxiliary flying squadrons ready to supplement the RAF and forty-two squadrons operating barrage balloons across the UK – these were also run by the AAF – and during the war were credited with destroying 279 V-1 flying bombs. At its peak in 1944 there were more than a hundred auxiliary squadrons.

During the Battle of Britain, the AAF provided fourteen out of a total of 62 fighter squadrons and accounted for almost thirty per cent of enemy kills. Any losses sustained by Fighter Command were backfilled largely via the RAFVR. The achievements of the AAF during WW2 did not go unnoticed and in 1947 HM King George VI approved the prefix 'Royal'.

After the war, the Royal Auxiliary Air Force (RAuxAF) were kept busy helping with the Berlin Airlift and participating in a number of NATO air exercises, but eventually all RAuxAF squadrons were disbanded in March 1957. A couple of years later the RAuxAF reappeared with the formation of three Maritime Headquarters Units and a Maritime Support Unit but nothing more happened with them until the late 1970s when the RAuxAF commenced a slow expansion culminating in April 1997 when the Royal Air Force Volunteer Reserve were fully amalgamated into the RAuxAF.

During 2003, the RAuxAF was involved in its first large-scale mobilization since the Korean War when almost 1,000 personnel were called up to support RAF operations overseas. There are currently twenty-five RAuxAF squadrons in the UK, which are continuing Trenchard's vision of providing trained professional backup resources to the regular RAF across many different roles.

Founded: 9 October 1924

Motto: *Comitamur Ad Astra*
(We go with them to the stars)

Notable AAF firsts

The first German aircraft shot down over the British mainland – 28 October 1939

The first 'kill' of a V-1 flying bomb – 14/15 June 1944

The highest score of any British night fighter squadron – 604 Squadron (127 victories)

Group of pilots from City of London 601 Squadron of the Auxiliary Air Force

12 The RAF Roundel

The famous RAF Roundel was originally devised during WW1 when it became apparent that markings of some kind were needed on aircraft in order to avoid confusion between enemy and friendly machines. To this end, orders were issued at the end of August 1914 for the Union Flag to be painted on the underside of the lower wings on all British aircraft. This indeed worked well when the aircraft were at low altitude, but as soon as they started to fly a bit higher the Union Flag was often mistaken for the German cross. Because of this, it was decided to adopt the French identification style of concentric circles, but with the red and blue rings swapped over. A miniature version of the Union Flag was painted between the circles and the wing tips and also on the rudder.

In May 1915, the Union Flag on the rudder was replaced by red, white and blue vertical stripes and in June an extra roundel was painted on the top surface of the upper wing. These roundels and stripes have formed the basis for British aircraft identification for over a hundred years. The design has evolved over the years and has seen subtle colour changes in order to reflect some of the various aircraft roles and their theatre of operation.

The Evolution of The Roundel

Union Flag (1914) – The original way of identifying British aircraft was to paint the Union Flag on the underside of the lower wings. But this led to misidentification at high altitude with the German Maltese Cross.

Royal Flying Corps (1914-18)
Copying the French Air Service method of identification but reversing the colours, this roundel was introduced to RFC and RNAS aircraft on 12 November 1914

RNAS (1914-15) Originally used on RNAS aircraft but this was stopped when it was decided to use the same identification as found on RFC machines.

Night Flying (1916-1918)
As aircraft began to operate at night a white ring was added to the aircraft to help identify them in the dark – although this was only rarely used.

Night Bomber (1918-38)
As camouflage was more prevalent in aircraft design and paintwork the original white and blue night flying roundel was modified to remove the white altogether and make the blue more prevalent with a red centre.

Royal Air Force (1920-39)
During the inter-war years the RAF used the standard roundel first displayed by the Royal Flying Corps in 1916.

RNAS (1915) As a short term measure, a blue dot was added to the original RNAS markings until the Royal Flying Corps roundel could be transferred to all RNAS aircraft.

RFC (1916-18) In 1916 brighter versions of the colours were used to aid identification.

RFC (1916-18) On machines that were painted in camouflage paint, an extra white circle was created around the outside of the roundel so it could be seen better.

Upper Wing design (1937-45) Just before the war the night bomber roundel was painted on the top of all aircraft wings.

Early Second World War (1939-41) The standard inter-war (1920 – 39) roundel with a yellow ring added to make identification of friendly aircraft easier.

Night Flying (1939-42) Painted on any RAF bomber that operated at night As well as the fuselage of all night fighters.

Fuselage (1942-47) Painted on all RAF aircraft fuselages, also appeared on the top of the wings of selected aircraft such as photo-reconnaissance Spitfires.

Underwing (1942-47) Used on aircraft which had light surfaces on the bottom of the wing.

South East Asia Command (1942) The standard fuselage roundel but with the red removed to avoid all confusion with Japanese aircraft.

South East Asia Command (1942-45) An improved version of the previous roundel. The two tone blue roundel made it easier to distinguish between friendly and hostile aircraft.

Royal Australian Air Force (1942-45) With a number of Royal Air Force aircraft helping the RAAF to defend Australia they also had the same roundel to aid identification.

Post War Roundel (1945) This was originally designed as the post war roundel for the RAF but was ultimately rejected.

Royal Air Force (1947 onwards) The standard RAF roundel.

V-Force (1955-64) Used on the trio of V-Force bombers (Vulcan, Victor, Valiant) when they were painted anti-flash white.

Low Visibility (1970 onwards) Used since 1970 on aircraft painted with camouflage design.

Modern roundel (1990 onwards) With moden aircraft largely painted grey this low visibility colour scheme was introduced in 1990.

Modern Training - This roundel is similar to the original RFC roundel of 1916 with a white outline and is used on all RAF training machines.

Stealth roundel – This is the roundel to be used on the new F35B Lightning II. Rather than simply painted on, this roundel will be incorporated into the actual design of the aircraft.

13 The Largest Airforce in the World

By the end of WW1 the Royal Air Force was the largest and most formidable air force in the world.

27,000
officers

= 1,000 men

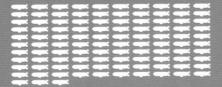

103
airships

22,500
aircraft

= 10 aircraft

401
aerodromes

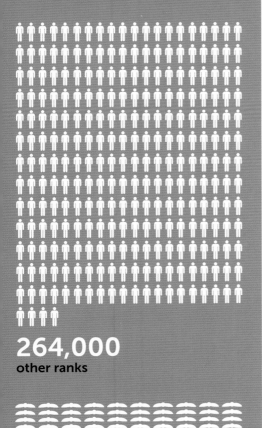

264,000
other ranks

75
**training
squadrons**

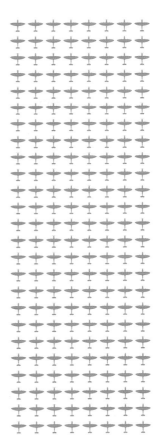

**At the outbreak of WW2,
in September 1939, the
operational strength of
the RAF in Europe had
diminished to about**

2,000
aircraft

＋ **= 10 aircraft**

14 The RAF Ensign

The Royal Air Force Ensign is the official flag of the RAF and is currently flown above every Royal Air Force station. The ensign was introduced in 1921, but not without controversy and opposition, especially from senior members of the Royal Navy.

Ever since its inception in 1918, officials of the Royal Air Force wanted their own flag or ensign, but the Royal Navy, who had the right to veto any new flag proposal that was to be flown within the British Empire (including on any ships or aircraft), actively rejected the idea. The Air Council continued to push the issue until the Admiralty reluctantly conceded, as long as it adopted the Union Flag with some appropriate design added.

These design views differed slightly to what the Air Ministry had in mind. They submitted a white ensign minus the St George cross, but this was immediately rejected by the Royal Navy as the white ensign (as well as the blue and red ones)

How not to use the Ensign

The RAF Ensign is never displayed except properly mounted on a staff or mast

As an ensign, it is not permitted to be carried on a parade nor may it be used as a decoration

It should not be draped over a coffin at a funeral; the appropriate flag for that purpose being the Union Flag

Size Matters

The size of the ensign flown is usually 3ft by 6ft (0.91m x 1.82m). On days when a formal inspection is to take place, an ensign twice this size is flown

were reserved for sole use by the Royal Naval Services.

Further designs were submitted and rebuffed by the Admiralty. Even the public got wind of the issue and started to submit their own designs, although none were adopted.

The idea of somehow using the roundel in the design had been discussed on and off for a while in the Air Ministry and it was suggested to add the Union Flag to the upper left of the design to give the mark of British authority. Lord Trenchard submitted the design to King George V who quickly approved it, as did the Admiralty.

The Ensign was officially introduced in December 1920 and on 24 March 1921 the King signed an Order in Council, thus defining its status and protecting it for authorised use.

15 Bomber Command

When RAF Bomber Command was initially formed in the summer of 1936, it was argued that a strong bomber force would provide a deterrent to unwanted aggression, as bombing would result in complete and inescapable destruction on both sides. In the early days Bomber Command was a limited and relatively ineffective force, but soon grew into a weapon of immense destructive power.

At the outbreak of WW2, Bomber Command consisted of twenty-three operational squadrons with just 280 aircraft. This modest force was only able to strike at carefully selected military targets such as airfields, ports and factories. Those early raids were also conducted during the day, resulting in heavy losses at the hands of enemy fighters.

In 1940, after the fall of France, Bomber Command began night-time bombing raids against German industrial targets, especially those factories producing synthetic oil. However, due to the lack of aircraft available and the difficulty in identifying targets meant these raids were of limited success.

1942 was a turning point for Bomber Command for two main reasons. The introduction of a new heavy bomber, the Avro Lancaster, and a new leader in the shape of Air Marshall Sir Arthur Harris. Harris was instrumental in lifting the restrictions on bombing individual targets to focus on breaking the will of German workers. Primary targets included the cities of Dortmund, Essen, Düsseldorf and Cologne, which was the target of the first 'Thousand Bomber Raid' during the night of 30/31 May 1942. As well as these massive city raids, other more specialised operations took place. The famous Dam Busters raid of May 1943 surprised the world with its ingenuity; the attack of the battleship *Tirpitz* in 1944 severely dented the *Kriegsmarine's* effectiveness to wage a sea war; and raids against the launch sites of German V-Weapons saved many British civilian lives.

Bomber command continued to operate successfully after the end of WW2. In 1956 over 100 Bomber Command aircraft took part in operations against Egypt during the Suez Canal crisis. By WW2 standards, the scale of attack was light but nonetheless effective. During the 1960s Bomber Command's famous 'V-Bombers' carried Britain's nuclear deterrent through challenging times until eventually relieved of this duty by Royal Navy submarines.

On 30 April 1968, Bomber Command was merged with Fighter Command to form Strike Command.

Avro Lancaster B Mark I, R5620 'OL-H', of No. 83 Squadron RAF, leads the queue of aircraft waiting to take off from Scampton, Lincolnshire, on the 'Thousand-Bomber' raid to Bremen, Germany 1942

Founded: 14 July 1936

Motto: *Strike Hard Strike Sure*

Headquarters: RAF Uxbridge (1936-40) RAF High Wycombe (1940-68)

WW2 Squadrons: 126 (32 of these were officially non-British units)

WW2 Sorties flown: 376,795

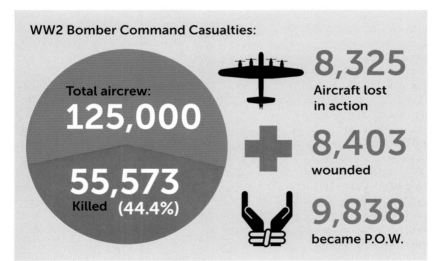

WW2 Bomber Command Casualties:

Total aircrew:
125,000

55,573
Killed (44.4%)

8,325
Aircraft lost in action

8,403
wounded

9,838
became P.O.W.

"From four miles up, I could clearly see the streets and buildings, many of which were burning fiercely. Huge blotches of red and green markers - dropped by our Pathfinder planes - mingled with the red and yellow flashes of exploding bombs."

Russell Margerison – mid upper gunner, Lancaster Bomber, 625 Squadron, RAF

16 Fighter Command

With tension in Europe rising in the mid-1930s, the RAF took the decision to split into four separate commands – Fighter Command, Bomber Command, Coastal Command and Training Command. The division formally took place on 14 July 1936 and the newly established Fighter Command was placed under the command of Air Marshall Hugh Dowding and headquartered at Bentley Priory on the outskirts of London.

Fighter Command was organised into a number of groups, set up to defend particular geographical areas of the country. Within each group were numerous stations where operational aircraft were based. The south-east of England was defended by 11 Group, the Midlands and East Anglia by 12 Group, and the north of England was patrolled by 13 Group. Later, and in response to threats posed to shipping, 10 Group was set up in the south west and 9 Group was formed to cover the north west and 14 Group looked after Scotland.

The key to Fighter Command's success was the operational control and communication systems that were in place. Information on incoming German attacks received from the Royal Observer Corps and various radar stations around the country were sent to Bentley Priory. Special map rooms were set up to allow the accurate plotting of incoming enemy aircraft and the Fighter Command forces

sent up to intercept. The commanders at Bentley decided on which group to involve and, once activated, the individual group commander would have complete control over which of his units he would scramble.

In addition to the fighter units and the Observer Corps, Dowding also inherited the Balloon Command and, in November 1938, the Anti-Aircraft system, the HQ of which was also at Bentley Priory.

The Operations Room at RAF Fighter Command's No. 10 Group Headquarters, Rudloe Manor

Dowding set about slowly updating the aircraft of Fighter Command, replacing many of the obsolete bi-planes with the fast and modern Spitfire, Hurricane and others. In 1939, only twenty-two of the thirty-five Fighter Command Squadrons had modern aircraft. By June 1940, Dowding could boast forty-eight squadrons almost all of which were equipped with the most up-to-date machines available. Dowding also made the most of the Auxiliary Air Force (AAF), the Women's Royal Air Force (WRAF) and the RAF Volunteer Reserve to expand the capability of Fighter Command. By the time the Battle of Britain roared into life in the summer of 1940 Dowding had succeeded putting together one of the best equipped and most efficient elements of the British war effort.

By the autumn of 1942, the arrival of the USAAF 8th Air Force and its daylight bombers would add bomber escort to Fighter Command's task, although a lack of combat range within most of the fighters, especially the Spitfire, meant such protection was limited to the Channel and the European coast. In 1943, Fighter Command was split up into the Air Defence of Great Britain and the Second Tactical Air Force that would focus on supporting ground forces after the eventual invasion of Europe.

After the war, Fighter Command was still primed to protect and defend Britain, but rather from Russia instead of Germany. With Russian bombers now having the option of carrying a nuclear bomb, the role of Fighter Command was as important as ever and a stream of new jet fighters entered service including the Meteor, Hunter and the Lightning.

In the 1957 Defence White Paper the government practically declared Fighter Command obsolete in the face of new unmanned missile technology and as a result investment was significantly cut. In 1961 Fighter Command was assigned to NATO's air defence system and in 1968 Fighter Command and Bomber Command merged together to form a new fighting force – Strike Command.

Founded: 14 July 1936

Motto: *Offence Defence*

Headquarters: RAF Bentley Priory

Disbanded: 30 April 1968

WW2 Casualties:

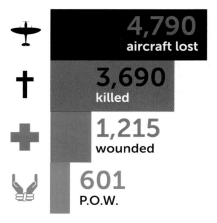

4,790 aircraft lost

3,690 killed

1,215 wounded

601 P.O.W.

Fighter Command Groups

Fighter Command was organised into a number of groups, set up to defend particular geographical areas of the country. Within each group were numerous stations where operational aircraft were based.

14 Group
HQ: Drumrossie Hotel, Inverness
Formed: 20 July 1940

13 Group
HQ: Kenton, Tyne and Wear
Formed: 24 July 1939

9 Group
HQ: Barton Hall, Preston
Formed: 9 August 1940
Disbanded: Mid 1944

12 Group
HQ: Hucknall, Notts
Formed: 14 July 1936

10 Group
HQ: Rudloe Manor
Formed: 1 June 1940
Disbanded: April 1945

11 Group
HQ: Hillingdon House, Uxbridge
Formed: 14 July 1936

17 Strike Command

RAF Strike Command was formed on 30 April 1968 through the merger of Bomber Command and Fighter Command. Signals Command was incorporated on 28 November 1969 and Air Support Command was absorbed on 1 September 1972. These mergers and acquisitions made it the largest single command in the RAF, controlling most of the available front line aircraft including strike/attack, reconnaissance, airborne early warning, maritime, air-to-air refuelling and transportation aircraft.

During the Cold War, Strike Command also held a strong NATO role and, in the case of war with the Soviet Union, Strike Command would have immediately assumed control over all RAF units as well as the US Third Air Force (based at RAF Mildenhall) as well as any further reinforcements that arrived in from the US or Europe.

Around the turn of the twenty-first century the RAF Strike Command enjoyed an established strength of around 28,000 service personnel along with 5,800 civilian staff — almost fifty per cent of the total strength of the RAF — and supported operations directly in many areas such as the Gulf, Kosovo and Afghanistan.

In 2007, Strike Command was merged with Personnel and Training Command to form a new single command — Air Command.

Founded: 30 April 1968

Motto: *Defend and Strike*

Headquarters: RAF High Wycombe

Groups: 9 active groups plus the Royal Observer Corps

The Lightning was Britain's first, and only, Mach 2 fighter. It could outfly and outfight any of its peers on entering service, and the maximum climb rate of 50,000 feet a minute was not equaled by a Western fighter until the F-15 entered service in 1976

Strike Command Strength (2005):

More than

500	**28,000**
aircraft	service personnel
across	
42	**5,800**
stations	civilian staff

18 Biggin Hill

Biggin Hill is perhaps the most famous fighter station in the world. It is definitely an iconic airbase renowned for its pivotal role in winning the Battle of Britain despite the *Luftwaffe's* best efforts to raze it to the ground.

The airfield was actually first operational in January 1917 when the Royal Flying Corps established a wireless testing area there during WW1. During the interwar years it remained an active venue for the RAF as they continued to test radio communication equipment on site.

At the beginning of WW2, two squadrons of Hurricanes were stationed at Biggin Hill along with a squadron of twin-engine Blenheim bombers, but as it quickly became obvious that Biggin Hill was going to be right in the front line of enemy air attacks the station became home to six squadrons although they were hardly ever operational at the same time.

The fighters stationed at Biggin Hill formed part of the defensive ring that protected Kent and Sussex. Initially they were used to proactively attack enemy aircraft over the south east coastal areas; they enjoyed some decent success which highlighted the station as a direct threat to the *Luftwaffe*. On 12 August 1940, the German bombers commenced their attacks on Biggin Hill. The first few attacks were relatively small scale but over the following days they increased in intensity, culminating in two huge attacks on 30 August which destroyed practically every building on the base.

Hurricanes from Biggin Hill went into combat for the first time on 21 November 1939 when two fighters intercepted and shot down a Dornier 17 just off of the Kent coast.

There was precious little protection for the staff and thirty-nine people were killed with another twenty-four wounded.

Despite the carnage and chaos Biggin Hill kept running. Teams of labourers were brought in to repair the runways and an emergency operations room was set up in the local village shop so that sorties could continue. Every effort was made to camouflage aircraft and pilots were housed in shops all over the village. The bravery and courage of the air base staff and crew was exemplified by three members of the Women's Auxiliary Air Force who continued to man the phones despite being in grave danger and repeatedly ordered to take cover in shelters. Elspeth Henderson,

Elizabeth Mortimer and Helen Turner were all awarded the Military Medal for their devotion to duty. Only six MMs were awarded to members of the WAAF throughout the entire war.

On 30 November 1940, two Spitfires scrambled without orders to try and shoot down the station's 600th enemy aircraft. A group of enemy Me109s were spotted over Deal and one enemy plane was shot down.

After the war Biggin Hill was used by RAF Transport Command, but in 1958 it was converted to an officer selection centre which ran until 1992. These days Biggin Hill is a civilian airport.

On 18 August, the Luftwaffe launched a major attack on Biggin Hill. In just ten minutes, 500 bombs were dropped and the base was severely damaged. By late afternoon, the base was back up and running.

"When the bombing of Biggin Hill got bad — the officers' mess was bombed — we were moved into temporary accommodation which was a sort of prefab. Then Fighter Command became nervous that there were three squadrons on the airfield so they said that we couldn't live on the airfield at night and we were billeted in country mansions three miles from the airfield."

Pilot Officer Tony Bartley, 92 Squadron, RAF

19 Coastal Command

Coastal Command was formed on 14 July 1936 alongside Bomber Command and Fighter Command. The primary tasks of Coastal Command were to protect Allied sea convoys and shipping from enemy attack – whether that be U-boats or air attack – and protect British coastline and ports from seaborne attack. However, it was never really given a crystal-clear mandate and always played third fiddle to its more prestigious cousins at both Bomber and Fighter Commands. As a result, when war was declared in 1939, RAF Coastal Command was far from ready. It only had 171 operational aircraft.

In 1940, once Germany had occupied France, Denmark, Norway and the Low Countries, Allied merchant shipping and British coastal regions were now under direct threat from enemy attack. Coastal Command was simply not up to the job; they couldn't protect merchant shipping and Fighter Command had to step in to help.

On 15 February 1941, Coastal Command was placed under the operational control of the Admiralty and eventually the command were given the resources and investment it needed. Modern radar and the latest long-range aircraft were delivered to help Coastal Command take the fight to the U-Boats and by May 1943, known as 'Black May' by the Germans, Coastal Command had begun to take the initiative and in the last few years of

the war they sank more U-boats than any other Allied service.

After the war, Coastal Command was reduced rapidly down to a minimal peacetime force although kept busy in various parts of the world including the Middle East and Palestine, it was also heavily involved in the Berlin Airlift.

The command was deemed too expensive to maintain, and cost cuts were made during the 1950s that caused a huge reduction in strength – by mid-1958 it possessed just sixty-seven aircraft. In the 1960s Coastal Command's focus turned to Russia's Northern Fleet, which demanded continual monitoring as they conducted operations in the Atlantic. Despite several encounters there was no recorded official confrontation.

Coastal Command was eventually disbanded on 2 October 1969 when it was merged into RAF Strike Command.

Founded: 14 July 1936

Motto: *Constant Endeavour*

Headquarters: RAF Northwood

Disbanded: 27 November 1969

Coastal Command completed over

1,000,000

flying hours
in WW2
across

240,000

separate
operations

A Short Sunderland on patrol

366

German
transport
vessels
sunk

212

U-boats
destroyed

5,866

personnel killed
in action

2,060

aircraft lost

10,663

people were
rescued including

5,721

Allied aircrew

Over 2000 gallantry
awards were
bestowed upon
Coastal Command
personnel during
WW2. Including four
Victoria Crosses, 17
George Medals and
82 Distinguished
Service Orders

20 RAF Search and Rescue Force

After the formation of the RAF in April 1918 it inherited a large fleet of support vessels originally part of the RNAS that were designed to support RAF seaplane operations. These vessels, ranging from pinnacles, lighters, launches, motorboats, depot ships and others were grouped together to form the Marine Craft Section (MCS).

During WW2, the MCS found itself woefully inadequate. During the Battle of Britain an RAF airman who was forced to ditch into the sea, only had a twenty per cent chance of getting back to their squadron. Considering this, on 6 February 1941 the RAF created the Directorate of Air Sea Rescue. Operationally it would become known as Air Sea Rescue Services (ASRS) and have the motto 'The sea shall not have them'.

By the end of the war it was the largest air rescue fleet in the world and more than 8,000 aircrew and 5,000 civilians had been saved.

In the 1950s, helicopters began to replace the fixed-wing aircraft and supplement the marine craft due to their ability to hover in one place whilst recovering survivors, and in the 1960s the RAF introduced the iconic Westland Wessex and Sea King helicopters that were to serve right up to its recent disbandment.

By 1986 the majority of the MCS marine craft were too old for service and were subsequently retired. From then on the RAF's rescue operations were solely helicopter based and consequently the group was renamed the Search and Rescue Force (SARF).

In 2006, the UK government announced plans to privatise the provision of search and rescue operations as part of a plan to replace the ageing Sea King fleet and on 4 October 2015 the Search and Rescue responsibilities of SARF were handed over to the Maritime & Coastguard Agency and Bristow Helicopters Ltd. The RAF's final search and rescue air operation took place on the same day, after Devon & Cornwall police asked for assistance in taking a thirty-eight-year-old man found unconscious on Ilfracombe Beach to a hospital.

On 18 February 2016, the disbandment of SARF was officially marked with a parade in front of the Duke and Duchess of Cambridge.

A RAF Search and Rescue Force Sea King in action

Founded: 6 February, 1941

Motto: *The sea shall not have them*

Headquarters: Northwood (along with RAF Coastal Command)

Disbanded: 4 October, 2015

SAR Force personnel have earned the highest number of non-combat gallantry awards given to any RAF unit including six George Medals and more than 50 Air Force Crosses.

Since records began in 1983 RAF SARF helicopters in the UK have responded to

34,122
callouts

Life-saving assistance has been given to

26,916
people

"The course has been challenging but I have enjoyed it immensely... I absolutely love flying, so it will be an honour to serve operationally with the search and rescue force, helping to provide such a vital emergency service."

Flight Lt William Wales (HRH Prince William, Duke of Cambridge) on his graduation as an RAF SARF rescue pilot, 17th September 2010

21 The Defence Whitepaper 1957

In 1957, the newly appointed Defence Minister, Duncan Sandys, issued a whitepaper which set forth his vision of the future of British military forces. It was to have a far-reaching affect on Britain's defence industry over the next decade and a somewhat demoralising effect on the RAF.

Ten days before Sandys became Defence Minister, the Soviet Union launched the Sputnik satellite – the first human made object to be launched into space. It was a momentous occasion that shocked the world, launched the space-race and ushered in new scientific and technological developments centred around missiles. It is not surprising then that the political view of that time was that Britain should move away from a defence system based on a show of large military strength and depend more on a strategic nuclear deterrent.

Of particular interest to the RAF was the idea that all manned aircraft could be replaced by guided missiles by 1970. With this philosophy at its foundation, the whitepaper surmised that all existing military aircraft development projects should be cancelled. It continued to stipulate that the RAF could survive with a regular strength of 135,000 men, and a fighter plane strength of just 280 (compared to the 480 in service in 1957). The RAF's bomber force could be completely replaced with ballistic missiles supplemented by American missiles. Coastal Command would be reduced from twelve to seven squadrons and Transport Command was to be reduced to seven and a half squadrons. Many overseas detachments would be dramatically cut or removed altogether including Germany and Hong Kong.

The paper also stated that the aircraft industry should re-organise and made it clear that any new contracts would only be given to firms that had merged together. In 1960, English Electric, Bristol Aeroplane Company and Vickers-Armstrongs merged together to form the British Aircraft Corporation (BAC). This new firm won the only new aircraft project going at the time – the doomed TSR2. In the same year de Havilland, Blackburn Aircraft and Folland were brought into the Hawker Siddeley company, whilst Westland Aircraft took control of all the remaining helicopter manufacturers. After all of these forced mergers of companies that were one-time competitors, the once buoyant British aircraft industry was never really the same.

One of the main drivers of these new proposals was the financial situation Britain found herself in after the conclusion of WW2. Britain was on the verge of bankruptcy and had become heavily dependent on US aid. This meant all areas of government were searching for areas where savings could be made and Sandys saw a cost-efficient missile programme as one such way to ease the financial crisis, despite the ramifications for the RAF.

Bloodhound Missile ▶

The 1957 Whitepaper 'at a glance'

- British defence strategy should centre around a strategic nuclear deterrent rather than old-fashioned military showmanship

- All manned aircraft could be replaced by guided missiles by 1970

- As a result almost all military aircraft development projects were to be scrapped

- RAF to be reduced to 135,000 men and 280 fighter planes

- Bomber Command to be replaced with ballistic missiles

- Costal Command and Transport Command to be severely reduced

- Overseas RAF posts to be removed completely or reduced

- British aircraft industry to re-organised with smaller firms merging together

22 Royal Air Force Aerobatic Team

Although the Royal Air Force Aerobatic Team (better known as the Red Arrows) was formed in late 1964 they were not the first RAF display team to take to the skies. RAF squadrons have been performing unofficially since 1920, but it was decided to pull them all together into an official unit in 1964 as RAF leaders were worried that pilots were spending too much time practising loop-the-loops than in actual operational training. The name 'Red Arrows' was an amalgamation of elements from previous display teams – the Black Arrows and the Red Pelicans – whilst the aircraft they would fly (the Gnat) was previously used by the Yellowjacks.

The first Red Arrows display was a press event at Little Rissington on 6 May 1965. By the end of the year they had flown in sixty-five displays across Europe and been awarded the Britannia Trophy by the Royal Aero Club for their contribution to aviation.

After 1,292 shows in the Gnat it was replaced in 1980 with the BAE Systems Hawk (essentially a training aircraft) which is still flying with the Red Arrows today. The Hawk flown by the Red Arrows is essentially the same as those flown by Advanced Flying Training students with the exception of modifications to produce the famous colourful trails and a slightly uprated engine.

The Red Arrows have displayed for fifty-three consecutive seasons and are an important part of a wider political statement, offering a unique capability to promote the UK abroad. For example, in 2016 they undertook a nine-week Middle and Asia-Pacific tour covering seventeen different countries. During the tour the Red Arrows drew crowds of over a billion people including huge crowds in China that were seeing them perform for the first time.

Red 6 and Red 7, the Synchro Pair perform a thrilling opposition pass during a Red Arrows display at the RAF Waddington International Airshow

By the end of the 2017 season the Red Arrows have been flying for...

53
seasons

4,900
displays in...

The greatest number of displays flown in any year is

136
in 1995

57
countries

Founded: 1964

Motto: *Éclat* (English: Excellence)

Headquarters: RAF Scampton

Size: 9 pilots & 91 support staff

During the team's world tour in 1995/96 the Red Arrows performed to nearly

1,000,000
people in Sydney on Australia Day

Ray Hanna AFC and Bar

In 1968 Squadron Leader Ray Hanna expanded the team to 9 planes, establishing the now famous 'Diamond Nine' formation. Hanna served as leader for four seasons and for his achievements with the team was awarded a Bar to his Air Force Cross.

Colourful trails

The famous smoke trails the team produce while flying are made by releasing diesel into the exhaust; this quickly vaporises, then re-condenses into very fine droplets, producing a white smoke trail. Dyes are then added to produce the red and blue colour. Each aircraft can carry enough diesel and dye to create five minutes of white smoke, one minute of red and one minute of blue during the display.

23 Hugh Montague Trenchard – The Father of the RAF

Often described as the Father of the RAF, Hugh Trenchard began his military career in the army, gaining a commission with the 2nd Royal Scots Fusiliers before being given a cavalry command during the Boer War. Severely wounded in the lung and spine on 5 October 1900, he needed significant recuperation before returning to South Africa for a second tour. After the war he went across to Nigeria, returning to Britain due to ill health in 1912.

Seeking a new challenge, he took flying lessons and, although not a world beating pilot, he was made adjutant of the Central Flying School. When war was declared he quickly took command of the First Wing of the RFC working closely with the then Lieutenant-General Sir Douglas Haig who commanded the First Army. The two leaders formed a strong and close working relationship and Trenchard was much admired by Haig, maybe because in those early days, Trenchard focused much of the RFC's efforts on clearing the way for, and giving support to, the ground forces of the army. This was achieved through the provision of aerial reconnaissance, tracking enemy movements and helping the artillery pinpoint targets, as well as attacking enemy rail and road networks and infantry formations.

While in charge of the RFC, Trenchard was obsessed with claiming (and maintaining) air superiority via aggressive offensive actions. At the best of times this meant losses to both men and machines, but in late 1915 when the Germans introduced a forward firing synchronised machine-gun into its Fokker fighters the older RFC machines were often cut to pieces. Despite this, Trenchard continued to repeat his orders day after day to keep flying over enemy lines to take the war to Germany. His only compromise was that his fighters should fly in groups to help defend each other. The gamble just about paid off and once new aircraft such as the FE2.B arrived at the front line, the momentum gradually swung back in Trenchard's favour – just in time for the 'Big Push' of summer 1916.

In order to keep pilots' morale high, Trenchard developed a policy of replacing all casualties on the same day they were lost. A reserve pool of pilots and observers were held at St Omer and moved to wherever needed to ensure a full complement of pilots for each squadron every morning.

It was a simplistic and slightly brutal approach which didn't always go down too well with his pilots, but it seemed to work and by the end of 1916 the RFC had more than proved itself. In June 1918, he was given the responsibility of organising the newly Independent Air Force and although he had grand plans of bombing key German industrial towns there were simply not enough bombers to carry out his ideas.

Post war, as Chief of the Air Staff, he fought hard to justify the continued independence of the RAF, he also founded the RAF College at Cranwell and set up an aircraft apprentice scheme. He introduced short-service commissions to provide a pool of ready-trained personnel should war ever loom large again. Tactically, Trenchard pushed the idea that Britain could only be properly defended by offensive bombing campaigns, although he seemed to have largely ignored the defensive options offered up by decent fighter squadrons. He was appointed as the first Marshall of the RAF in 1927, stepping down in 1930 to take up a role as Commissioner of the Metropolitan Police. At the outbreak of WW2 he was repeatedly offered senior posts in an effort to tempt him back into the armed services, but he refused them all, although did act as an unofficial Inspector General to the RAF.

Regarded by many as 'the father of the RAF', Hugh Trenchard died on 10 February 1956 in London at the age of eighty-three.

> Trenchard built up a reserve pool of pilots and observers who were held at St Omer in order to fulfil his desire that there was always "a full breakfast table, with no empty chairs."

> "Trenchard often came to visit us at Treizennes, particularly during the period of our heaviest casualties. Although it was partly as a result of his aggressive policy in the air that we were having those shocking losses, it must not be thought that he was unaware of, or indifferent to what was happening to us. Trenchard was very deeply concerned about that, but it did not change his opinion about what should be done..."

Major William Sholto-Douglas, 43 Squadron, RFC

63

24 Captain A.G. 'Sailor' Malan and his Ten Rules for Air Fighting

Adolph Gysbert Malan DSO & Bar, DFC & Bar (better known as 'Sailor' Malan) was a South African fighter Ace who lead No 74 Squadron, RAF during the Battle of Britain who ended up with 27 confirmed kills, seven shared destroys, three probable destroys and sixteen damaged.

Malan was an aggressive pilot and an exceptional shot but above all he was an astute tactician in the art of dog-fighting and spent a lot of time teaching the younger pilots that came into his Squadron. Malan developed a set of simple rules for fighter pilots to follow, eventually these 'Ten Rules' were cascaded down throughout RAF Fighter Command and could be seen displayed on the walls of many Fighter Squadrons and training schools.

Malan survived the war, returning back to South Africa where he was a prominent figure in the fight against apartheid.

Group Captain A G "Sailor" Malan - 1943

27 Confirmed kills

1. Wait until you see the whites of his eyes. Fire short bursts of one to two seconds only when your sights are definitely "ON".

2. Whilst shooting think of nothing else, brace the whole of your body: have both hands on the stick: concentrate on your ring sight.

3. Always keep a sharp lookout. "Keep your finger out".

4. Height gives you the initiative.

5. Always turn and face the attack.

6. Make your decisions promptly. It is better to act quickly even though your tactics are not the best.

7. Never fly straight and level for more than 30 seconds in the combat area.

8. When diving to attack always leave a proportion of your formation above to act as a top guard.

9. INITIATIVE, AGGRESSION, AIR DISCIPLINE, and TEAMWORK are words that MEAN something in Air Fighting.

10. Go in quickly – Punch hard – Get out!

25 Pauline Gower

Pauline Gower gained her pilots licence on 4 August 1930 after only fifteen hours of flying time. She had just turned twenty and had achieved this at a time when very few women were able to drive, let alone fly a plane. However, this wasn't enough for Pauline, she wanted to earn a living from flying, which meant she needed to get a commercial licence. She enrolled at the London Aeroplane Club and was awarded her commercial (or B licence) on 13 July 1931. She was only the third woman in the world to earn a commercial pilot's licence.

Shortly afterwards, Pauline, along with fellow female aviator Dorothy Spicer, started the first all-female air taxi and joy ride service, based out of a field in Kent. During the early thirties, Britain was going crazy for air travel and the business boomed. She also performed at air shows up and down the country and was beginning to make a name for herself in aviation circles, although it was not always plain-sailing.

She was fined £222 in 1933, having taxied her Spartan into a stationary Moth at Cardiff while giving joyrides in an air pageant (although she reckoned it had definitely moved since she checked where it was). Three years later, she was taken to hospital suffering from concussion and 'lacerations of the scalp' after she collided with another aeroplane on the ground, this time at Coventry airport.

During her air-taxi career, she was reckoned to have piloted more than 33,000 passengers.

Over the years, she became a sought after speaker and was invited to serve on numerous committees, one of which was concerned with air safety. In 1939 she was given a Commission in the Civil Air Guard.

By this time, it was obvious that war was practically inevitable. As the RAF started to ready itself it was also obvious that it needed more pilots. Women were not allowed to fly in the RAF at that time, but with more than 2,000 flying hours under her belt, Gower was determined to try and help the war effort however she could. At the same time, Gerald d'Erlanger was busy forming the Air Transport Auxiliary, a service that would use pilots not eligible for RAF service but who could still be useful transporting mail, supplies and spare parts from factory to airfield. In an effort to recruit pilots for the ATA, letters were sent out to all civilian pilots with more than 250 hours' flying experience. Pauline was asked to head the Women's section of the ATA.

At the beginning of the war there were only nine female pilots in the ATA, however under her leadership and guidance as Commandant of the Women's Section of the Air Transport Auxiliary, that number grew steadily to more than 150 women, flying all kinds of machines from single-seat trainers to massive heavy bombers such as the Lancaster.

In recognition for her service to the war effort she was awarded the MBE in 1942. The following year she was appointed a director of BOAC – probably the first woman in the world to be appointed to the board of any civilian airline.

Tragically she died in 1947 giving birth to her twin sons.

The first eight female pilots were appointed to the ATA on 1st January 1940. By the end of the war it had recruited 168.

"Some people believe women pilots to be a race apart, and born 'fully fledged'. Women are not born with wings, neither are men for that matter. Wings are won by hard work, just as proficiency is won in any profession."

Pauline Gower in 'A Harvest of Memories', P.170 (Sept 1995)

Pauline Gower at the controls of a de Havilland Tiger Moth

26 Group Captain Sir Douglas Bader, CBE, DSO & Bar, DFC & Bar

Bader on his Hurricane at Duxford 1940

Douglas Bader was born in St John's Wood, London, on 21 February 1910 and spent the early years of his life in India before returning to the United Kingdom. His uncle was adjutant to the Royal Air Force College at Cranwell and, like many young men of that generation, he was keen to make a living flying. He joined the Royal Air Force in 1928, won a scholarship to Cranwell and graduated in 1930.

After graduating he was posted to No. 23 Squadron flying the Gloster Gamecock. However, on 14 December 1931, he crashed a Bristol Bulldog at Woodley aerodrome, near Reading, while doing some low level aerobatics, apparently as

a dare, and was seriously injured in the process. Both of his legs were amputated as a result.

Within six months Bader had learnt to walk unaided with his 'tin legs' and in June 1932 was back in the cockpit when it was arranged for him to pilot an Avro 504 to see if he could still fly. He could, and a subsequent medical suggested he was fit for active duty. Despite this, the RAF decided not to reinstate him and Bader was invalided out in May 1933.

In the summer of 1939, aware that war was inevitable, Bader set out to re-join the RAF. He easily passed tests at the Central Flying School and then undertook a refresher course before joining No. 19 Squadron in February 1940, based at Duxford. Here he first flew the Supermarine Spitfire, undertaking convoy patrols but without seeing action. A switch to No. 222 Squadron, also at Duxford, brought action over Dunkirk in June 1940 and on the 24th he was promoted to Squadron Leader and given command of No. 242 Squadron, a Hawker Hurricane unit based at RAF Coltishall. This squadron was made up mainly of Canadian pilots and had suffered high losses during the Battle of France. Morale was low and they took time to accept their new commanding officer, but he soon won them over with his energetic and charismatic style of leadership. It was not long before the squadron was back up to strength and found itself in the thick of the Battle of Britain where Bader proved himself a fine fighter pilot and an inspirational leader. By the end of the Battle his unit had claimed sixty-two victories and for his role he was awarded the Distinguished Flying Cross.

In March 1941, Bader was promoted to Wing Commander and was now stationed at RAF Tangmere. Bader led his wing on numerous 'sweeps' of northwest Europe and bomber escort missions. He continued to rack up more enemy 'kills' until his tally reached an impressive twenty. However, on 9 August 1941, he collided with a Bf 109 over France and was forced to bail out of his Spitfire losing one of his artificial legs as he leapt from the aircraft. He was taken prisoner by the Germans who gave special permission for a new prosthetic to be dropped to him by air, promising they would not shoot down a delivery aircraft.

As a prisoner of war, Bader made it his mission to be as painful to his captors as possible. He attempted to escape numerous times, in fact he made so many attempts that the Germans threatened to take away his legs. Eventually they moved him to Colditz Castle where he was liberated in April 1945.

After returning to the UK, Bader was promoted to Group Captain and took control of the Fighter Leaders School, and then the North Weald fighter sector. In September 1945, he was given the honour of leading the first Battle of Britain flypast before finally leaving the RAF in March 1946.

He was appointed Commander of the Order of the British Empire (CBE) in 1956 and knighted in 1976 – both decorations were to recognise his work with disabled people.

Sir Douglas Bader died in 1982 aged seventy-two. In his memory, his family set up the Douglas Bader Foundation which works hard to advance and promote the physical, mental and spiritual welfare of persons who are without one or more limbs, or otherwise physically disabled.

"Don't listen to anyone who tells you that you can't do this or that. That's nonsense. Make up your mind you'll never use crutches or a stick, then have a go at everything. Go to school, join in all the games you can. Go anywhere you want to. But never, never let them persuade you that things are too difficult or impossible."

Sir Douglas Bader

27 The Letter that changed history

During the spring of 1940 the Germans were running riot in France and the Low Countries. A handful of RAF bombers plus six squadrons of Hurricanes were stationed across France in an effort to stem the tide of the German advance, but they were getting smashed.

On 15 May Holland surrendered. On the same day Churchill agreed to send four more Hurricane squadrons over to France to reinforce the current garrison. This decision was against the will and better judgement of Air Chief Marshall Sir Hugh Dowding, who openly confronted Churchill, pulling from his pocket a graph depicting recent Hurricane losses. As he pointed at the red line that moved in a steep downward curve, he explained to the Prime Minister in no uncertain terms that if the line continued at the same rate for another ten days there would be no Hurricanes left to defend England or France.

Despite this, the very next day Churchill agreed to let France have ten new fighter squadrons. When Dowding found out about this new promise he channelled his anger and fears by way of a letter, written on 16 May 1940 at RAF Bentley Priory. Dowding knew that to successfully defend Britain from air attack he would need fifty-two fighter squadrons and he was already down to thirty-six. In the letter he put forward his views on how moving more squadrons to France would put the safety of Britain at serious risk.

He handed the letter to his Chief Civil Servant for delivery to the War Cabinet who scanned it and said, 'You know that Churchill will have to read this?' to which Dowding simply replied, 'I know, that's why I wrote it.'

Dowding was immediately summoned to the War Cabinet Room at 10 Downing Street to discuss the situation with the Prime Minister as well as Sir Archibald Sinclair who had been recently appointed as the new Air Minister, Lord Beaverbrook who had just received his appointment as Minister for Aircraft Production and Sir Cyril Newhall who was the Chief of Air Staff. Dowding stood by his view despite Churchill reminding him of the promise he had made to France, to which Dowding replied, 'I am well aware of the situation Prime Minister, but my task at hand is for the air defence of this country and it is my belief that I cannot achieve this if half my aircraft are in France.'

The letter worked, Churchill agreed on a compromise of six squadrons of Hurricanes to be sent to France, but they were to operate from bases on the Northern French coast next to the Channel, this way they could return to British bases quickly if needed.

With the Battle of Britain just around the corner, this was a vital partial-victory. Dowding's letter has since been described as the letter that changed the course of history.

Telephone Nos: WATFORD 9241 (10 lines)
                COLINDALE 5221 (4 lines)
                PINNER 5691 (3 lines)

Telegraphic Address: " AIRGENARCH, STANMORE "

Reference: FC/S:19048.

HEADQUARTERS FIGHTER COMMAND,
ROYAL AIR FORCE,
BENTLEY PRIORY,
STANMORE,
MIDDLESEX

<u>SECRET</u>

Sir,

I have the honour to refer to the very serious calls which have recently been made upon the Home Defence Fighter Units in an attempt to stem the German invasion on the Continent.

2. I hope and believe that our Armies may yet be victorious in France and Belgium, but we have to face the possibility that they may be defeated.

3. In this case I presume that there is no-one who will deny that England should fight on, even though the remainder of the Continent of Europe is dominated by the Germans.

4. For this purpose it is necessary to retain some minimum fighter strength in this country and I must request that the Air Council will inform me what they consider this minimum strength to be, in order that I may make my dispositions accordingly.

5. I would remind the Air Council that the last estimate which they made as to the force necessary to defend this country was 52 Squadrons, and my strength has now been reduced to the equivalent of 36 Squadrons.

6. Once a decision has been reached as to the limit on which the Air Council and the Cabinet are prepared to stake the existence of the country, it should be made clear to the Allied Commanders on the Continent that not a single aeroplane from Fighter Command beyond the limit will be sent across the Channel, no matter how desperate the situation may become.

7. It will, of course, be remembered that the estimate of 52 Squadrons was based on the assumption that the attack would come from the eastwards except in so far as the defences might be outflanked in flight. We have now to face the possibility that attacks may come from Spain or even from the North coast of France. The result is that our line is very much extended at the same time as our resources are reduced.

8. I must point out that within the last few days the equivalent of 10 Squadrons have been sent to France, that the Hurricane Squadrons remaining in this country are seriously depleted, and that the more Squadrons which are sent to France the higher will be the wastage and the more insistent the demands for reinforcements.

9. I must therefore request that as a matter of paramount urgency the Air Ministry will consider and decide what level of strength is to be left to the Fighter Command for the defences of this country, and will assure me that when this level has been reached, not one fighter will be sent across the Channel however urgent and insistent the appeals for help may be.

10. I believe that, if an adequate fighter force is kept in this country, if the fleet remains in being, and if Home Forces are suitably organised to resist invasion, we should be able to carry on the war single handed for some time, if not indefinitely. But, if the Home Defence Force is drained away in desperate attempts to remedy the situation in France, defeat in France will involve the final, complete and irremediable defeat of this country.

I have the honour to be,

Sir,

Your obedient Servant,

Air Chief Marshal,
Air Officer Commanding-in-Chief,
Fighter Command, Royal Air Force.

28 "The Few" Speech by Winston Churchill

Sir Winston Churchill's extraordinary reputation (including being voted as the greatest ever Briton in a 2002 BBC poll) is in no small part down to his defiant leadership during the darkest days of the Second World War. Churchill had an incredible ability to inspire the people around him, not just other leaders and politicians, but also the general public at large – and he did this, through his speeches. One of his most inspirational and iconic speeches of the war was delivered on 20 August 1940 as the Battle of Britain continued to be played out across the skies of Britain. This speech is remembered for one single sentence:

```
Never in the field of human
conflict was so much owed by
some many to so few.
```

Historians continue to debate whether 'The Few' are indeed Fighter Command as presumed by so many, or indeed Bomber Command which is the subject for the majority of the rest of the speech. It could just be a catch-all phrase for the entire RAF. We will probably never know. What we do know, however is that it galvanised a nation and brought home to the wider public that Fighter Command was playing David to Germany's Goliath – they found the concept of 'the few' a fitting testament to British heroism.

Churchill had always had a keen interest in air power and was involved in some of the strategic thinking behind the Royal Naval Air Service during the First World War, especially some of the long-distance bombing raids against German airship bases.

A few days before he made the famous 'Few' speech, on 16 August 1940, Churchill, with his Chief-of-Staff, General Ismay, called in on the HQ of 11 Group at Uxbridge, and watched as he committed all of his fighters in the defence of this country. As they left, Churchill told Ismay, "Don't speak to me; I have never been so moved." It is as they both got in the car to leave that Churchill muttered "Never in the field of human conflict was so much owed by so many to so few". Although in a post-war interview, General Ismay recounts that Churchill's first form of the sentence was "Never in human history was so much owed by so many to so few" but it was changed after Ismay replied "What about Jesus and his disciples?"

Churchill's role in the summer of 1940 was to rally support for the continuation of the war and give the public evidence of British defiance and fortitude in the face of a stronger enemy – and even though throughout the majority of the Battle of Britain the RAF actually had more men and machines than the *Luftwaffe*, he succeeded.

An excerpt from the 'The Few' speech - 20th August 1940.

The great air battle which has been in progress over this Island for the last few weeks has recently attained a high intensity. It is too soon to attempt to assign limits either to its scale or to its duration. We must certainly expect that greater efforts will be made by the enemy than any he has so far put forth... It is quite plain that Herr Hitler could not admit defeat in his air attack on Great Britain without sustaining most serious injury. If after all his boastings and bloodcurdling threats and lurid accounts trumpeted round the world of the damage he has inflicted, of the vast numbers of our Air Force he has shot down, so he says, with so little loss to himself ...if after all this his whole air onslaught were forced after a while tamely to peter out, the Fuhrer's reputation for veracity of statement might be seriously impugned. We may be sure, therefore, that he will continue as long as he has the strength to do so...

...It must also be remembered that all the enemy machines and pilots which are shot down over our Island, or over the seas which surround it, are either destroyed or captured; whereas a considerable proportion of our machines, and also of our pilots, are saved, and soon again in many cases come into action... We believe that we shall be able to continue the air struggle indefinitely and as long as the enemy pleases, and the longer it continues the more rapid will be our approach, first towards that parity, and then into that superiority, in the air upon which in a large measure the decision of the war depends.

The gratitude of every home in our Island, in our Empire, and indeed throughout the world, except in the abodes of the guilty, goes out to the British airmen who, undaunted by odds, unwearied in their constant challenge and mortal danger, are turning the tide of the World War by their prowess and by their devotion. Never in the field of human conflict was so much owed by so many to so few. All hearts go out to the fighter pilots, whose brilliant actions we see with our own eyes day after day, but we must never forget that all the time, night after night, month after month, our bomber squadrons travel far into Germany, find their targets in the darkness by the highest navigational skill, aim their attacks, often under the heaviest fire, often with serious loss, with deliberate, careful discrimination, and inflict shattering blows upon the whole of the technical and war-making structure of the Nazi power. On no part of the Royal Air Force does the weight of the war fall more heavily than on the daylight bombers who will play an invaluable part in the case of invasion and whose unflinching zeal it has been necessary in the meanwhile on numerous occasions to restrain....

29 Sir Arthur Harris

Sir Arthur Harris (known universally by his given nickname 'Bomber') led RAF Bomber Command during the height of the Allied strategic bombing campaign against Germany. For three years Harris pursued the systematic destruction of Germany from the air with an uncompromising determination, which has resulted in him being arguably the most controversial Allied commander of the war.

Born in Gloucestershire on 13 April 1892 he initially rejected his parents' wish of a military career and travelled to Rhodesia where he earned a living mining for gold, driving horses and farming. When war broke out in 1914, he joined the 1st Rhodesia Regiment and fought alongside South African forces in South West Africa. After the campaign came to an end in July 1915, he was discharged from the Rhodesian Regiment but he was still keen to take part in the war so travelled back to England. After failing to land a commission in the cavalry or the artillery, he joined the Royal Flying Corps on 6 November 1915. After learning to fly he served with distinction both on the Home Front and in France, where he gained a reputation for being something of a night-fighting pioneer. Harris claimed five enemy kills and was Awarded the Air Force Cross on 2 November 1918.

After the war, Harris stayed in the RAF and commanded several bomber squadrons across India and Iraq. He rose

quickly through the ranks and was in command of 5 Group by the time WW2 started, where he remained until he was appointed Deputy Chief of the Air Staff in November 1940. In February 1942, Harris was appointed as Commander-in-Chief of Bomber Command.

Harris quickly got to work on reinvigorating this largely under-achieving area of the RAF. At the time heavy losses of bombers on daytime raids and wildly inaccurate night-time raids had led to the suspension of long-range sorties by the RAF. New and improved aircraft (such as the Lancaster) along with bigger and better bombs, improved tactics and improvements to radar worked together to transform Bomber Command into one of the most potent weapons of war Britain possessed. In May 1942, he gathered together the maximum number of available bombers and devastated the German city of Cologne in the first of three 'thousand bomber' raids. These massive attacks were exactly what the deflated Bomber Command needed and quickly raised morale as well as helping to win much needed public support.

Harris was a great proponent of 'area bombing' and held the strong belief that massive and sustained bombing of Germany's industrial cities would force her to surrender. On a number of occasions he declared that the war would be over in a matter of months despite an increasing number of Allied leaders and politicians quietly distancing themselves from this strategy. Not surprisingly, Harris had very strong views on this subject and fiercely fought any attempt to transfer Bomber Command's resources into smaller precision-bombing activities. He was ordered to switch targets to railway and communication networks in the run up to D-Day, but after the invasion the strategic bombing campaign was resumed.

Perhaps the most controversial raids of the war involved the systematic destruction of the German city of Dresden that took place over four large raids between 13 and 15 February 1945. During these raids, 722 heavy bombers from the RAF, along with over 500 USAAF bombers, dropped almost 4,000 tons of explosives onto the city, causing a firestorm that practically destroyed Dresden and resulted in approximately 25,000 deaths. The raids sat uneasily with many people back in Britain, with members of the press calling it a 'terror raid' – even Churchill distanced himself from such action, writing in a memo in April 1945: We must see to it that our attacks do no more harm to ourselves in the long run than they do to the enemy's war effort.

Despite all the consternation, Harris was promoted to Marshal of the RAF in 1945, but retired from the service soon after the war ended, moving to South Africa to run an international shipping business before returning to the UK in 1953. Harris died on 5 April 1984, eight days before his 92nd birthday.

In 1992, a statue to Harris was unveiled near Trafalgar Square in London. Within twenty-four hours, red paint was poured over it – such was/is the controversy surrounding his bombing tactics.

"Attacks on cities like any other act of war are intolerable unless they are strategically justified. But they are strategically justified in so far as they tend to shorten the war and preserve the lives of Allied soldiers. To my mind we have absolutely no right to give them up unless it is certain that they will not have this effect. I do not personally regard the whole of the remaining cities of Germany as worth the bones of one British Grenadier."

After the Dresden raids, Harris defended his actions strongly in a memo written in February 1945

30 The top ten RAF Aces of World War 1

Pilot:	Kills:	Awards:	Notes:
William Avery "Billy" Bishop	**72**	**VC, CB, DSO & Bar, MC, DFC MiD, ED (Canada) Légion d'honneur (Fr) Croix de Guerre (Fr)**	Top Canadian and British Empire Ace.
Edward Corringham "Mick" Mannock	**61**	**VC, DSO & 2 Bars, MC & Bar**	Top British Ace Killed in Action 26/7/1918
Raymond Collishaw	**60**	**CB, DSO & Bar, OBE, DSC DFC, MiD (4 times), Order of St Anna 2nd Cl w/swords (Ru), Croix de Guerre (Fr)**	The highest scoring Ace of the RNAS and the first pilot to score six victories in one day.
James "Mac" McCudden	**57**	**VC, DSO & Bar, MC & Bar, MM Croix de Guerre (Fr)**	Started his RFC career as a mechanic but became the most highly decorated British born airman of WW1. Killed in an air accident on 9/7/1918

Pilot:	Kills:	Awards:	Notes:
Andrew Beauchamp-Proctor	54	VC, DSO, MC & Bar, DFC, MiD	Killed on 21/6/1921 in an air accident.
Donald MacLaren	54	DSO, MC & Bar, DFC, Legion d'Honneur (Fr) Croix de Guerre (Fr)	Helped with formation of the Royal Canadian Air Force in 1919/20
William George "Billy" Barker	50	VC, DSO & Bar MC & Two Bars MiD (3 times) Croix de Guerre (Fr), 2x Silver Medal of Military Valour (It)	With 12 gallantry awards he is the most decorated serviceman in Canada's history.
Robert A. Little	47	DSO & Bar, DSC & Bar, MiD Croix de Guerre (Fr)	The most successful Australian flying ace of the war. Killed in Action 27/5/1918
George McElroy	47	MC & 2 Bars DFC & Bar	The leading Irish fighter Ace in the war. Killed in Action 31/7/18
Albert Ball	44	VC, DSO & 2 Bars MC, MiD, Legion d'Honneur (Fr) Order of St. George (Ru)	Killed in Action 7/5/17 aged just 20. At the time of his death he was Britain's leading flying Ace.

30 The top ten RAF Aces of World War 2

Pilot:	Kills:	Awards:	Notes:
Marmaduke "Pat" Pattle	At least **40**	**DFC & Bar**	Killed 20th April 1941 over Athens.
James "Johnnie" Johnson	**34**	**DSO & 2 Bars DFC & Bar, CB CBE, DFC (USA) Air Medal (USA) Legion of Merit (USA) Croix de Guerre (Bel) Cmdr of the Legion d'Honneur (Fr)**	The most successful British pilot. All kills were against enemy fighters.
Pierre Clostermann	**33**	**Grand Croix of the Legion d'Honneur Croix de Guerre DSO DFC & Bar DSC (USA) Silver Star (USA) Air Medal (USA)**	Flew with the Free French Air Force. Also flew several hundred missions against V-1 rocket launch sites.
George "Buzz" Beurling	**31**	**DSO DFC DFM & Bar**	The most successful Canadian fighter pilot of the war. Known as the "Knight of Malta" having been credited with shooting down 27 Axis aircraft in just 14 days over the besieged Mediterranean island.

Pilot:	Kills:	Awards:	Notes:
William "Cherry" Vale	30	DFC & Bar AFC MiD	Achieved 20 kills while flying the Hawker Hurricane and 10 with the Gloster Gladiator making him the second highest scoring Hurricane and biplane pilot in the RAF, in both cases after Marmaduke Pattle.
Robert Tuck	29	DSO DFC & 2 Bars AFC, MiD DFC (USA)	Hit by anti-aircraft fire on 28th January 1942, was forced to land in France and was taken prisoner for the rest of the war.
John "Bob" Braham	29	DSO & 2 Bars DFC & 2 Bars AFC, Order of the Crown (Bel), Croix de Guerre (Bel)	19 of his 'kills' came at night making Braham one of the most accomplished night fighter pilots of the RAF.
Brendan "Paddy" Finucane	At least 28	DSO DFC & 2 Bars	There are several conflicting records as to his total tally at the end of the war. Could be as high as 32. KiA on 15th July 1941 aged just 21.
James "Ginger" Lacey	28	DFM & Bar MiD Croix de Guerre (Fra)	The second highest scoring RAF fighter pilot of the Battle of Britain.
Adolph "Sailor" Malan	27	DSO & Bar DFC & Bar Cross de Guerre (Bel) War Cross (Cz), Legion d'Honneur (Fr), Croix de Guerre (Fr)	South African fighter pilot who saw action at Dunkirk, The Battle of Britain and D-Day.

31 RAF Slang

Arse-end Charlie
The man who weaves backwards and forwards above and behind the squadron to protect them from attack

Line shooter
Someone boasting or telling tall tales (shooting a line)

Brolly
Parachute (from the appearance of the 'chute when fully opened)

Job
An aircraft. *A very fast German job came out of nowhere*

Sprog
A young recruit someone recently promoted. *Sprog Corporal*

Rocket
A severe reprimand. *Getting the rocket*

Sack of taters
A loadful of bombs, delivered all at once

Camp comedian
A Camp Commandant

Irons
Knife, fork, spoon (short for eating irons)

Spit and polish parade
A parade inspection by a C.O.

Brock's benefit
A very bright/intense display of flares, searchlights and anti-aircraft fire

Ham-bone
A Hampden Bomber

Beehive
A close formation of bombers (the hive) with a fighter escort (the bees)

Scarlet slugs
Anti-aircraft gun tracer fire

Bus driver
A bomber pilot as he often travelled the same route

Insy
Incendiary bomb

Kipper kites
Planes protecting shipping convoys in the North or Irish seas

Half pint hero
Someone who rarely goes into action but talks and boasts a lot

Cabbage
A bomb. *To sow one's cabbages* is to drop one's bomb load

Happy valley
An area of land frequently bombed. Such as the Ruhr

Spout
The barrel of a gun. *Make sure you have one up the spout ready, chaps*

Supercharged
Drunk

Soup
Dirty, foggy weather

Gone for a Burton
Dead or missing

Attaboy
A member of the Air Transport Auxiliary – many of whom were American

Met
Meteorological Officer

Wop
Wireless Operator

Hurry
A Hurricane fighter plane

Joy stick
The control lever of an aircraft

Tail-end Charlie
Nickname given to the rear gunner

Sid Walker gang
A crash salvage party

Get up them stairs
A phrase often told to a married man who is about to go on leave

Blood Wagon
Ambulance

Schooly
Education Officer

Hip flask
Revolver

Hop the twig
To fatally crash

Stooge
A deputy, stand-in or assistant

Snake
A lively or noisy party. *We are out on the snake tonight* – at a party

Silver Sausage
Barrage balloon

Binders
Aircraft brakes

Aviate
To show off while flying

31 More RAF Slang

Banana boat
An aircraft carrier

Mae West
The safety jacket
worn by pilots and
aircrews

Muscle Merchant
A PT Instructor

Niff-naff
Excessive fuss or
procrastination.
*Don't niff-naff, get
cracking!*

Off the beam
To make a mistake.
*I was off the beam
there, sorry*

Topside
Flying, airborne

Visiting card
A bomb

Bang on
Perfection. *We
dropped our bombs
bang on the target*

Messer
A Messerschmitt

Old Newton
The force of gravity,
always tending to
pull a plane to earth

The old man
The Commanding
Officer

Pathfinder
An airman who is
adept at finding
ladies to party with

Three pointer
A perfect landing –
on all three points
(the wheels)

Wimpey
Wellington Bomber

Bag
To shoot down

Go to the movies
Going into action

Nursery
Flying school

Office
A plane's cabin
or cockpit

Paraffin Pete
An officer, or NCO
engaged in Airfield
Control

Taps
The controls, buttons
and indicators etc in
the cabin/cockpit of
a plane

Tin fish
A torpedo

Wopag
A wireless operator and air gunner. *Taken from the official abbreviation W.Op/A.G.*

Waafery
The officer or billets of the W.A.A.F. (Women's Auxiliary Air Force)

Pulveriser
A nickname for the Stirling Bomber as it could carry very heavy bombs

Groupy
Group Captain

Gravy
Aviation fuel

Full bore
Flying at maximum speed

Chocks away
Let's get started

Whistle
To take off quickly in order to attack or intercept the enemy

Wingco
Wing Commander

Shed
Aircraft hangar

Scramble
To take off

Queen Bee
The W.A.A.F. officer in charge

Joe Soap
Name given to an airman who is doing work that should be done by another

The fizzer
A detention room or punishment room at camp

Wheels down
To get ready (to leave a train or bus). Taken from the lowering of wheels in preparation for landing

Scrub around
To take evasive action. From the circular motion of scrubbing

The drink
The sea. *After being shot down he was forced to ditch his plane into the drink*

Fireworks
Heavy Anti-Aircraft fire

Bogey
An enemy aircraft

Belly
The undercarriage of an aircraft

Moments
of Courage

Victoria Cross

Descripton:

A cross pattée bearing the crown of St Edward surmounted by a lion, with the words FOR VALOUR inscribed underneath on a semi-circular scroll. The suspension bar is decorated with laurel leaves.

Ribbon:

38mm wide. Originally naval crosses (including RNAS) used a dark blue ribbon, with army and air crosses having crimson ribbon. Since 1918 all awards use the crimson ribbon.

Eligible Recipients:

Awarded to any member (regardless of rank) of the UK, Commonwealth, or UK territory Armed Forces whose actions demonstrated the most conspicuous bravery, or some daring or pre-eminent act of valour or self-sacrifice, or extreme devotion to duty in the presence of the enemy.

Metal:

Bronze, originally from Russian guns captured in the Crimea, although other guns from other conflicts have also been used.

Reverse:

A circular panel in the centre of the back of the cross in which is engraved the date of the act for which the VC was awarded. On the reverse of the suspension bar is engraved the details of the recipient.

VC Awards by service:

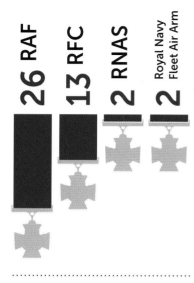

26 RAF

13 RFC

2 RNAS

2 Royal Navy Fleet Air Arm

During WW2 only 1 VC was awarded to Fighter Command.

No RAF personnel have been awarded the Victoria Cross since the end of WW2.

VC awards by conflict:

World War 1 — **19**

World War 2 — **22**

William Barnard Rhodes – Moorhouse was the first RFC aviator to be awarded the Victoria Cross after he was killed in action in April 1915

VC Awards to Overseas services under RAF Command

2 Royal New Zealand Air Force

2 Royal Australian Air Force

2 Royal Canadian Air Force

1 Royal South African Air Force

33 Victoria Cross recipients
World War 1

Name:	Squadron	Date of action
William Barnard Rhodes – Moorhouse	No 2 Squadron, RFC	26 April 1915
Reginald Alexander John Warneford	No 1 Squadron, RNAS	7 June 1915
Lanoe George Hawker	No 6 Squadron, RFC	25 July 1915
John Aiden Liddell	No 7 Squadron, RFC	31 July 1915
Gilbert Stuart Martin Insall	No 11 Squadron, RFC	7 November 1915
Richard Bell-Davies	No 3 Squadron, RNAS	19 November 1915
Lionel Wilmot Brabazon Rees	No 32 Squadron, RFC	1 July 1916
William Leefe Robinson	No 39 Squadron, RFC	2-3 September 1916
Thomas Mottershead	No 20 Squadron, RFC	7 January 1917
Francis Hubert McNamara	No 67 (Aust) Sqdron, RFC	20 March 1917
Albert Ball	No 56 Squadron, RFC	25 April to 6 May 1917
William Avery Bishop	No 60 Squadron, RFC	2 June 1917
James Thomas Byford McCudden	No 56 Squadron, RFC	23 December 1917 to 2 February 1918
Alan Arnett McLeod	No 2 Squadron, RFC	27 March 1918
Alan Jerrard	No 66 Squadron, RFC	30 March 1918
Edward Corringham Mannock	No. 74 Squadron and No. 85 Squadron	17 June 1918 to 26 July 1918
Andrew Frederick Weatherby Beauchamp-Proctor	No. 84 Squadron	8 August 1918 to 8 October 1918
Ferdinand Maurice Felix West	No. 8 Squadron	10 August 1918
William George Barker	No. 201 Squadron (attached)	27 October 1918

34 Victoria Cross recipients
World War 2

Awarded postumously

Name:	Squadron	Date of action
Donald Edward Garland	No. 12 Squadron	12 May 1940
Thomas Gray	No. 12 Squadron	12 May 1940
Roderick Alastair Brook Learoyd	No. 49 Squadron	12 August 1940
Eric James Brindlay Nicolson	No. 249 Squadron	16 August 1940
John Hannah	No. 83 Squadron	15 September 1940
Kenneth Campbell	No. 22 Squadron	6 April 1941
Hughie Idwal Edwards	No. 105 Squadron	4 July 1941
Arthur Stewart King Scarf	No. 62 Squadron	9 December 1941
John Dering Nettleton	No. 44 (Rhodesia) Squadron	17 April 1942
Leslie Thomas Manser	No. 50 Squadron	30-31 May 1942
Hugh Gordon Malcolm	No. 18 Squadron	4 December 1942
Guy Penrose Gibson	No. 617 Squadron	16-17 May 1943
Arthur Louis Aaron	No. 218 Squadron	12 August 1943
William Reid	No. 61 Squadron	3 November 1943
Cyril Joe Barton	No. 578 Squadron	30 March 1944
Norman Cyril Jackson	No. 106 Squadron	26-27 April 1944
John Alexander Cruickshank	No. 210 Squadron	17-18 July 1944
Ian Willoughby Bazalgette	No. 635 Squadron	4 August 1944
Leonard Cheshire (Baron Cheshire)	Several bomber squadrons	1940 to 1944
David Samuel Anthony Lord	No. 271 Squadron	19 September 1944
Robert Anthony Maurice Palmer	No. 109 Squadron	23 December 1944
George Thompson	No. 9 Squadron	1 January 1945*

Distinguished Flying Cross

Bar:

A silver slide-on bar was added to the medal ribbon for additional acts of valour, for which a subsequent DFC was awarded.

Silver

Description:

A silver cross flory ending with a rose, surmounted by another cross of propeller blade. The cross is suspended from a bar featuring a sprig of laurel. On the reverse is the Royal Cypher in the centre with the year of issue engraved on the lower arm.

Ribbon:

30mm wide, originally horizonal alternate stripes of white and purple, changed after June 1919 to diagonal stripes.

Eligible Recipients:

Awarded to officers and warrant officers of the RAF for acts of valour, courage or devotion to duty shown during active operations against the enemy. From 1993 the DFC was available to both officers and other ranks.

Medals awarded:

World War 1
1,116

World War 2
20,354

Bars:

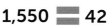

75 **3**

1,550 **42**

Only three men won 2 Bars to the DFC in WW1:
Captain Arthur Henry Cobby (Australia)
Captain Walter Hunt Longton (Britain)
Captain Ross MacPherson Smith (Australia)

65 DFC's were awarded between 1948 and 1952

Medals
Distinguished Flying Medal

Ribbon:

Originally purple and white horizontal stripes but since July 1919 thirteen diagonal stripes alternating white and purple

Bar:

A silver slide on bar was added to the medal ribbon for additional acts of courage, for which a subsequent DFM was awarded.

Silver

Eligible Recipients:

Awarded to aircrew, NCO's and men of the RAF for courage or devotion to duty while flying on active operations against the enemy. In 1993 the DFM was replaced by the DFC which is now awarded to all ranks.

Description:

An oval medal with the reigning sovereign's effigy on the obverse and an image of the goddess Athena Nike seated on an aeroplane, with a hawk rising from her hand, above the words 'For Courage' on the reverse. The medal is suspended by a pair of wings from a straight bar.

Medals awarded:

World War 1 **104**

World War 2 **6,638**

Bars: 1

58 1

Approximately 150 medals have been awarded since 1945.

The only person to receive two Bars to the DFM was 745707 Sergeant (later Wing Commander) Donald Earnest Kingaby DSO, AFC, DFM & Two Bars

Air Force Cross

Bar:

A silver slide-on bar was added to the medal ribbon for additional acts of valour, for which a subsequent AFC was awarded.

Silver

Ribbon:

30mm original horizontal stripes, but since 1919 diagonal alternate stripes of white and crimson

Eligible Recipients:

Awarded to officers and warrant officers of the RAF for gallantry on non-operational missions and for meritorious service on flying duties. Since 1993 it has been available to all ranks.

Description:

The cross consists of a thunderbolt, the arms conjoined by wings, surmounted by another cross of aeroplane propellers on which is inscribed the Royal Cypher. A central roundel depicts Hermes mounted on a Hawk bestowing a wreath.

Medals awarded:

World War 1 **678**

World War 2 **2,001**

Bars:

12 **3**

26 **1**

The only person to win the AFC three times (AFC & 2 Bars) in WW2 was Wing Commander H J Wilson

Medals
Air Force Medal

Ribbon:

Originally horizontal narrow stripes of white and crimson but since July 1919 diagonal narrow stripes of the same colour

Bar:

A silver slide on bar was added to the medal ribbon for additional acts of courage, for which a subsequent DFM was awarded.

Silver

Eligible Recipients:

Awarded to aircrew, NCO's and men of the RAF for courage or devotion to duty while flying, but not on active operations against the enemy. In 1993 the AFM was replaced by the AFC which is now awarded to all ranks.

Description:

An oval medal with a laurel border. On the obverse was the reigning sovereign's effigy and on the reverse is a representation of Hermes standing on top of a flying hawk, holding a laurel wreath. The medal is suspended by a pair of wings from a straight bar.

Medals awarded:

World War 1
102

World War 2
259

Bars:

2

95

Conspicuous Gallantry Medal (Flying)

Originally instituted on 15th August 1855 as an award for Naval and Marine NCO's and men. Extended out to RAF personnel on 10 November 1942

Bar:

A silver slide-on bar was added to the medal ribbon for additional acts of valour, for which a subsequent CGM was awarded silver rosette.

Silver

Ribbon:

Light blue with dark blue stripes on either side.

There were only 110 CGM (Flying) medals awarded. 109 of them were awarded during the Second World War. Only two men have won a bar to the CGM (Flying): Flight Sergeant Norman Francis Williams and Warrant Officer Alan Penrose. 89 out of the 109 WW2 awards went to members of Bomber Command

Description:

The effigy of the reigning monarch on the obverse; on the reverse the words FOR CONSPICUOUS GALLANTRY in three lines within a crowned laurel wreath.

Eligible Recipients:

Awarded to aircrew, NCO's and men of the RAF for conspicuous gallantry shown during air operations against the enemy. The CGM (Flying) was second only to the Victoria Cross for operational flying against the enemy. As a result of the 1993 review this decoration has now been replaced by the Conspicuous Gallantry Cross.

38 Medals

The Air Crew Europe Star

Instituted 1945

Ribbon:

The centre of the ribbon is pale blue (representing the sky) with a narrow yellow stripe either side (enemy searchlights) with black edges (night flying).

Clasp:

If the recipient was serving at sea as part of a maritime air force and was awarded the Atlantic Star, the award of the Air Crew Europe Star was denoted by a clasp to the Atlantic Star

Bronze

Description:

A six pointed star with a circular centre. In the middle is the GRI / VI monogram, surmounted by a crown and inscribed with THE AIR CREW EUROPE STAR around the foot.

Eligible Recipients:

Awarded for operational flying over Europe for a minimum period of two months between 3rd September 1939 and 5th June 1944. Army personnel qualified for this star after they had served on air crew duties for four months, provided two months of this minimum four-month period had been operational flying over Europe with at least one operational sortie.

The award of a gallantry medal or Mention in Dispatches for action during operational flying over Europe qualified the recipient for an immediate award of the Air Crew Europe Star, regardless of service duration. Personnel whose required qualifying service period was terminated prematurely by their death, disability or wounding on active service were awarded the Star regardless of service duration.

The Battle of Britain clasp to the 1939/45 Star

Clasp:

A 'Battle of Britain' clasp was sewn directly onto the ribbon of the 1939-1945 Star. When just the ribbon was worn, the bar was represented by a gilt rosette.

Ribbon:

Equal stripes of dark blue, red and light blue symbolising the Royal Navy, Army and Royal Air Force respectively.

Bronze

Eligible Recipients:

The Battle of Britain clasp was awarded to RAF aircrew who took part in at least one operational sortie against the enemy whilst flying with one of the 71 squadrons of Fighter Command engaged in the battle between 10th July and 31st October 1940. This included crew-members of aircraft such as the Defiant & Blenheim, and not just pilots of Spitfires and Hurricanes. RAF ground crews who kept the Battle of Britain fighters in the air did not even qualify for the 1939-1945 Star, let alone the Battle of Britain clasp.

Description:

A six pointed star with a circular centre. In the middle is the GRI / VI monogram, surmounted by a crown and inscribed with THE 1939-1945 STAR around the foot.

2,937

British and Allied airmen were awarded the Battle of Britain clasp.

Medals

The Bomber Command clasp to the 1939/45 Star

Instituted
26 February 2013

Clasp:

A 'Bomber Command' clasp was sewn directly onto the ribbon of the 1939-1945 Star. When just the ribbon was worn, the bar was represented by a

Ribbon:

Equal stripes of dark blue, red and light blue symbolising the Royal Navy, Army and Royal Air Force respectively.

Bronze

Eligible Recipients:

The Bomber Command clasp was awarded (belatedly) to air crew members on aircraft who participated in at least one operational sortie in a RAF Bomber Command operational unit between 3rd September 1939 and 8th May 1945.

Description:

A six pointed star with a circular centre. In the middle is the GRI / VI monogram, surmounted by a crown and inscribed with THE 1939-1945 STAR around the foot.

A few months after the clasp was launched, The Ministry of Defence said it had received 2,165 applications from surviving Bomber Command veterans, it was widely reported in the press at the time that many veterans were disappointed that he government didn't recognise them with a full medal, instead of just a clasp.

Machine
Moments

40 Tiger Moth

In the early 1930s the RAF were using a handful of de Havilland DH.60 Moths as training planes, but they were not convinced about its suitability, specifically around the poor accessibility of the front cockpit. By this time all crew members wore parachutes as standard and getting in and out of the Moth – which meant clambering through all the wing struts and wires – was tricky enough when the plane was stationary on terra firma, but in the air this was practically impossible. As such the RAF went back to de Havilland and asked for a new improved version.

With the prospect of a nice big order from the RAF on the horizon, Geoffrey de Havilland got on the case right away; by literally dismantling an old Moth and putting it back together again in an improved fashion. The result was the Tiger Moth, perhaps one of the most iconic planes of RAF history to date.

Because the potential reward for such a machine was large, de Havilland had considerable competition from long forgotten machines such as the Robinson Redwing, the Blackburn Bluebird, the Avro Cadet and the Hawker Tomtit. However, after extensive trials at the Aeroplane and Armament Experimental Establishment at Martlesham Heath, the RAF ordered an initial batch of thirty-five DH.82 Tiger Moths.

The first production machines were delivered to the RAF Central Flying School in 1932. Those first trainers possessed a Gipsy III piston engine which delivered 120bhp but these were eventually replaced by a Gipsy Major I engine which upped the power to 130bhp and enabled the Tiger Moth to hit a top speed over just over 100mph, although its typical cruising speed was around 65–70mph. One of the reasons it was so successful as a trainer was that it wasn't quite as easy to fly as some of the other contenders – the Tiger Moth needed a confident pilot at the controls and in many ways it quickly highlighted piloting mistakes without endangering life – thus in the eyes of many an instructor, it was the perfect training machine.

By the time of WW2 the RAF had 500 Tiger Moths in operation but another 4,000 were built just for the RAF to help train up their WW2 pilots. All in all over 9,000 de Havilland Tiger Moths were built until it was eventually phased out of service in 1952 in favour of the the de Havilland Chipmunk.

Tony Hisgett/WikiCommons

Crew:

1

(+ 1 optional instructor)

Armament: None

Max Speed:

104

mph
(167 km/h)

Range:

300

miles (483km)

Service Ceiling:

14,000

feet (4,276m)

Numbers built:

9,000+

41 Short Sunderland

The Short Sunderland was the most important British-built aircraft to serve with RAF Coastal Command during WW2 and played a vital part in the Allied victory in the Battle of the Atlantic. The RAF received their first Short Sunderland in June 1938 and by the time of WW2 RAF Coastal Command were operating a fleet of forty. Their main duty was convoy protection and with it anti-submarine warfare. At first successes were few and far between – no aerial depth charges were available – and so the Sunderlands were armed with less than effective anti-submarine bombs. During 1940, the Sunderlands sank two U-boats (shared with Naval ships) and damaged a third, but during the whole of 1941 and 1942 they had no success at all.

That all changed in 1943 with the introduction of new radar systems that allowed Sunderlands to detect U-boats on the surface without being detected. Sunderlands accounted for five U-boats

in May 1943 alone. On 6 June 1944, Sunderlands were out in force protecting the D-Day invasion fleet from U-boat attack.

The final Coastal Command Sunderland operational mission was in June 1945 over four weeks after the German surrender. Long-range Sunderland operations also took place overseas from bases in Africa and the Far East.

Post-war, Sunderlands took part in the Berlin Airlift where ten aircraft supplied 4,920 tonnes of freight to the beleaguered city. During the Korean War, Sunderlands based in Japan undertook nearly 900 operational sorties totalling over 13,350 flying hours. The Sunderland's design was so good that it remained in front line service for over twenty years, with 749 machines built in total during this time. It was also the last flying-boat operated by the Royal Air Force. The Sunderland finally retired from RAF service in 1959.

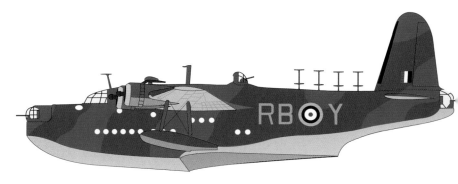

Living in the Sunderland

It was not uncommon for crews to live in their Sunderland between flights. If the aircraft was moored, two men were required to be on board during the night.

First U-boat success

The Sunderland's first U-boat victim was U-55. She had been damaged by surface warships, and was then attacked and forced to scuttle by Sunderlands of No.228 Squadron on 30 January 1940.

Flying Porcupine

Because of the many guns protruding from the aircraft, the Germans dubbed it the "Flying Porcupine"!

D-Day sinkings

On the night 6/7 June 1944 Sunderland's sank two U-boats (U-955 and U-970) while protecting the D-Day invasion fleet.

Max Speed:

210

mph
(340 km/h)

Crew:

9-11

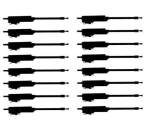

Armament:

16 Browning .303 machine guns

2 Browning 0.5 inch machine guns

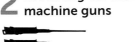

Range:

1,780

miles (2,848km)

Service Ceiling:

16,000

feet (4,800m)

42 Hawker Hurricane

Many of the fighter planes that were introduced in the late 1930s (such as the Supermarine Spitfire and the Messerschmitt Bf 109) were modern, innovative designs, yet the Hurricane was more of an evolution and was able to trace its lineage back to the Hawker Hart of 1928.

Ultimately the Hurricane was a safe design based on tried and tested technology and while it wasn't as advanced as the Spitfire, the Hurricane had a reputation for being ultra-reliable and incredibly tough. It could take a lot more punishment than most fighters and still bring its pilot home safely.

During the early 1930s the backbone of the RAF's fighter defence was the Hawker Fury – and it was indeed a formidable aircraft for its time. However, time was moving very quickly with regards to aircraft design and innovation and it was soon apparent that biplanes would be eclipsed by monoplanes. Following discussions with the Air Ministry, Hawker was allowed to submit a new design – called at that time the Hart Monoplane – and on 6 November 1935 the first prototype, fitted with a brand new Merlin C engine took to the skies.

The new plane was impressive with a top speed of 315mph – it also had some simple design features that would go a long way to helping build its future rugged reputation. It continued with an old style tubular fuselage covered in fabric, which meant that if shot, bullets would pass right through and repairs were simple. It also had a retractable undercarriage which, unlike the Spitfire, withdrew inwards creating a wider wheelbase making it much more stable during landing and taxiing.

The Air Ministry placed an order for 600 and the first production Hurricane, fitted with the new Merlin II engine, took to the skies on 12 October 1937 with the first four machines delivered to 111 Squadron just before Christmas that year. Back in the Hawker factory, design improvements were being worked on even though only a handful of production-ready Hurricanes were operational – all metal wings to increase performance and to help take the weight of the wing-mounted canons, a bullet proof windscreen for the pilot and a new propeller blade that increased speed by 17mph – machines with these new and improved specification were delivered to 111 Squadron in the spring of 1940.

The Hurricane proved its worth alongside the Spitfire during the Battle of Britain but within a couple of years it had been largely superseded by new and improved aircraft. The Hurricane took on many different roles during the war including night fighting and tank busting – the later meant that a 40mm anti-tank cannon was mounted under each wing. Churchill even agreed to supply Russia with Hurricanes to bolster the Russian Air Force.

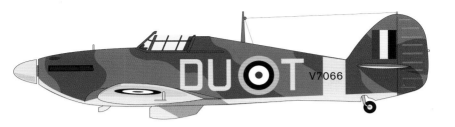

The only Fighter Command VC of WW2

While attacking a formation of Ju 88s over Southampton in his Hurricane on 16 August 1940, Flight Lieutenant James Nicholson's Hurricane was hit and badly damaged by an enemy Bf 110. His plane was on fire and just as he was about to exit his blazing machine he saw an opportunity to attack another Bf 110 so he re-entered his burning cockpit to attack it, finally bailing out only after he had destroyed this second enemy aircraft. He was wounded in the eye, the foot and suffered severe burns in the process. He was also shot at as he parachuted to the ground by members of the Home Guard. For this heroic action he was awarded the Victoria Cross — the only VC awarded to Fighter Command during WW2.

Crew:

1

Max Speed:

340
mph
(547 km/h)

Armament:

Initially 8x .303 Browning machine guns. Later version carried 4x20mm Hispano Cannon...

Range:

600
miles (965km)

Service Ceiling:

36,000
feet (10,970m)

Numbers built:

14,583

43 Supermarine Spitfire

The Spitfire was a machine that was adored by both its pilots and the public in equal measure and became a symbol of a nation determined to fight for its very survival. The Spitfire served in all of the RAF's operational theatres during WW2 and was engaged in active front line service for over twenty years. During this time 20,351 machines were produced in over twenty variations for many different roles, making it the most widely produced aircraft in RAF history.

When it first entered service in 1938, the Spitfire was the first all-metal monoplane in production as well as being the fastest machine in the RAF fleet. The Mk Vb, powered by a supercharged Merlin V12 engine, was capable of just over 370mph (595km/h) at a height of 35,000ft (10,668m). As the war progressed performance was continually enhanced and during the winter of 1943 a specially modified Spitfire clocked a remarkable 606mph or Mach 0.89!

Speed wasn't the only thing on the minds of the Spitfire's designers. Throughout the war the initial armament of eight .303inch Browning machine guns were replaced by up to four 20mm cannons, or a mixture of both. It was a machine that definitely packed a punch, but perhaps the Spitfire's greatest asset was its superior agility and responsiveness, meaning it was also able to evade enemy fighter planes and live to fight another day.

Spitfire production took some time to get going during the early war years and by the time the RAF were engaged in the Battle of Britain there were more Hurricanes in service than Spitfires. They also took more losses, mainly because they were detailed to take on the German Messerschmitt Bf 109 fighter plane whereas the Hurricanes were often asked to take out the German bombers.

By 1943 a 14,000 strong workforce (forty per cent of whom were women) were churning out 300 Spitfires a month. The plane played a major part in the Allied victory of WW2 and will probably remain the most iconic plane in the history of the RAF.

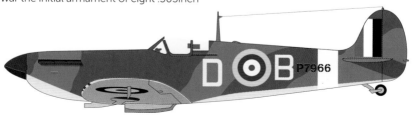

The Pilots

Training:

Officially 150 hours of flying tuition followed by 40 hours at an Operation Training Unit, however, at the height of the Battle of Britain some pilots saw action after just 10 hours flying experience.

"In my view the Spitfire was a much better aircraft than the Messerschmitt 109. The turning rate was fantastic compared to the 109. The climbing rate was also very good…"

Walter Krupinski – Messerschmitt 109 pilot

Kit:

Parachute pack

Leather flying helmet incorporating radio headphones

Goggles

Oxygen Mask

Silk scarf

Inflatable lifejacket (known as the Mae West)

Sheepskin flying jacket

Leather gloves

Leather boots

Average age:

20

Crew:

1

Max Speed:

371

mph
(597 km/h)

Armament:

2x20mm Hispano II Cannon / 4x 0.303 Browning Machine Guns / 2 x 250lb (113kg) or 1 x 500lb (227kg) bomb

Range:

470

miles (760km)

Service Ceiling:

35,000

feet (10,668m)

Numbers built:

20,351

44 AVRO Lancaster

Born from the unsuccessful Manchester bomber, the Avro Lancaster was without question Bomber Command's most iconic and successful heavy bomber of WW2. In December 1941, No. 44 (Rhodesia) Squadron took ownership of the first three production Lancasters and within three months they were ready for front line action.

On 3 March 1942, four Lancasters from No. 44 Squadron took part in their first operational raid with some minelaying off Heligoland on the north-west coast of Germany. A week later, two No. 44 Squadron Lancasters took part in their first bombing raid along with 124 other aircraft against the German industrial city of Essen.

Over the course of the war, the Lancaster took part in thousands of raids over enemy territory, flying 156,000 individual sorties. It also took part in a number of specialist raids such as the attack on the German Battleship *Tirpitz* in November 1944 and Operation *Chastise* in May 1943, better known as the Dam Busters raid.

Immediately after the war finished, Lancasters were used widely as a transport plane to bring back thousands of British PoWs from across Europe. The big bomber continued active service with Bomber Command in significant numbers until it was replaced by the Avro Lincoln. The final Bomber Command Lancaster was officially retired from service in December 1953.

Crew:
7

Max Speed:
287 mph
(462 km/h)

Numbers built:
7,377

Lost in action:
3,249

Armament:
8 Browning .303 machine guns

Range:
2,530 miles (4,072km)

Service Ceiling:
21,400 feet (6,500m)

Max bomb load:
1 x 22,000lb 'Grand Slam'' bomb
or 14,000lb (6,350kg) of smaller bombs

10

Lancaster crew members were awarded the Victoria Cross during WW2

"I would say this to those who placed that shining sword in our hands: Without your genius and efforts we could not have prevailed, for I believe that the Lancaster was the greatest single factor in winning the war."

Letter from Sir Arthur Harris, Commander in Chief of Bomber Command, sent to Sir Roy Dobson of A.V. Roe & Co. after the war

45 De Havilland DH98 Mosquito

Nicknamed 'the wooden wonder' the versatile DH98 Mosquito was without doubt de Havilland's greatest contribution to the war effort during WW2.

Originally designed as a long-range bomber that was able to carry a 6000lb bomb all the way to Berlin and back, the Mosquito saw active service as a fighter-bomber, night-fighter, trainer, torpedo-bomber, photo-reconnaissance plane, pathfinder and high-speed courier. During the first designs the de Havilland team decided to sacrifice the gun turrets to save weight and give the plane more speed – there were many concerns in the Air Ministry about the wisdom of an unarmed bomber, but de Havilland was convinced that Mosquito's speed would overcome its lack of firepower. The RAF seemed to agree, at least in principal, and placed an order for fifty Mosquitos on 1 March 1940. In an era where the American Flying Fortress bomber was armed to the teeth with machine-guns and had more turrets that you could shake a stick at, the unarmed Mosquito seemed, at least on paper, like a fish out of water, but little did they know that the Mosquito was actually way ahead of its time. In the future, bombers such as the Canberra, the Victor and Vulcan would not carry a single gun.

One year to the day after the end of the Battle of Britain, the DH98 Mosquito entered service. Yes, it was late to the party, but it was immediately successful and became well-known for its bombing, pathfinder and precision, low-level strike capabilities. Wartime development resulted in a wide range of variants (thirty-three) and a significant increase in bomb load capability and range due to the incorporation of a larger bomb bay and auxiliary fuel tanks.

The Mosquito carried out thousands of bombing raids with Berlin a common target, as it was one of the few bombers that had the range and carrying power to hit the German capital. Yet it was low altitude hit-and-run raids that caught the public's imagination – and the British media exploited these to their max as occasionally the RAF allowed special camera planes to accompany the real fleet on raids. One of the most famous hit-and-run raids on Berlin was timed to take place at the exact time Hermann Göring began a radio address celebrating the Nazi party's tenth anniversary. That speech had to be abandoned.

7,781 Mosquitos were built, the last one rolled off the production line on 15 November 1950. The Mosquito outlived its supposed successor, the de Havilland Hornet, by several months of RAF service. A bigger, better Merlin-powered 'Mosquito Series 2' was planned but never built, nor was the Super Mosquito concept which, on paper would have been able to carry an 8,000lb monster bomb at a speed of 430mph. In 1951, the Mosquito was replaced by the English Electric Canberra – another high speed, unarmed bomber.

"We believe that we could produce a twin-engine bomber which would have a performance so outstanding that little defensive equipment would be needed."

Geoffrey de Havilland – September 1939

Wooden Wonder

The fuselage of the Mosquito was built in two halves using a combination of laminated spruce, balsa wood and mahogany.

Nazi hit-and-run

A Mosquito daylight attack knocked out the main Berlin broadcasting station on the very day Hermann Göring was giving a speech to celebrate the 10th Anniversary of the Nazis' seizing of power.

Crew:

2 👤👤

Max Speed:

408 mph (657 km/h)

Range:

2,450 miles (4,540km)

Service Ceiling:

36,000 feet (11,000m)

Maximum bomb load of 2,000– 4,000lb (910– 1,810kg)

46 Gloster Meteor

Britain's first jet fighter and the only Allied jet aircraft to see combat during WW2, the Gloster Meteor, was a revolutionary aircraft whose development began in 1940 with a collaboration between the Gloster Aircraft Company and Power Jets Ltd – the company owned by Sir Frank Whittle, one of the early pioneers of jet propulsion.

The Meteor prototype first took to the air on 5 March 1943 powered by a pair of de Havilland H1 turbojet engines. Subsequent test flights used different jet engines to compare performance and reliability. Eventually, after issues with supply, Rolls Royce took over engine production and the first Meteors were delivered to the RAF in July 1944. No. 616 Squadron, based at RAF Culmhead, swapped out their Spitfires for Gloster Meteor F1 jet fighters to become the RAF's first ever jet squadron.

In January 1945, the Meteor F1 was replaced by the F3, this new version alleviated some of the technical issues found on the first production model – that same month some of 616 Squadron were relocated to operate with the RAF's Tactical Air Force over north-west Europe, although they were forbidden to fly over enemy territory in case one was shot down and captured by the Germans.

After the war, the F4 was introduced – it was almost 170mph (270kmh) quicker than the original version. It set a new world speed record of 606mph (975kmh) on 7 November 1945 and broke it less than a year later when it recorded 616mph (991kmh) on 7 September 1946.

Such performance made it very popular with international air forces and the Meteor was exported overseas in large numbers. However, by the late 1940s other aircraft had caught up in terms of performance so an new and improved version – the F8 – was introduced and would serve as the backbone of Fighter Command until the mid-1950s when it was transformed into an able night-fighter, remaining in service until 1961.

3,947 Meteors had been produced by the time production ceased in 1955, serving all over the world – some of which remained in service until the 1980s.

First combat victory for a British jet fighter

On 4 August 1944, a 616 Squadron Meteor, piloted by Flight Officer 'Dixie' Dean, destroyed a V1 flying bomb to register the jet fighter's first combat 'kill'.

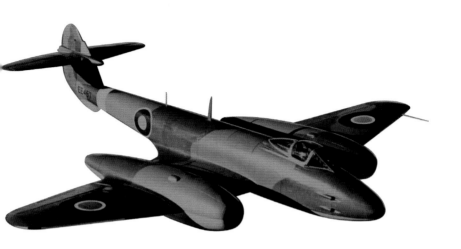

No jet-to-jet action in WW2

Although operational at the same time, the Meteor never engaged with the Messerschmitt Me262 – so there was no jet-to-jet fighting during WW2.

Crew:

1 🧍

Max Speed:

600
mph
(965 km/h)

Armament:

4 x 20mm Hispano MkV Cannon / upto eight 5inch HVAR rockets / two 1000lb bombs

Range:

600
miles (965km)

Service Ceiling:

43,000
feet (13,100m)

Numbers built:

3,947

47 English Electric Canberra

Originally designed to replace the Mosquito bomber after WW2, the English Electric Canberra is probably one of the longest serving and most versatile aircraft the RAF have ever put into service having been used in numerous different roles over an incredible fifty-four years.

With development commencing in the final months of WW2, the first prototype took to the skies in May 1949. Tests were so positive that the Canberra was sent into production almost immediately and the first service-ready aircraft were delivered in 1951. At that time, a top speed of 580mph meant the Canberra was capable of outrunning almost all other jet fighters designed to intercept her. Originally the design only supported the Canberra carrying bombs in the internal payload area, but subsequent designs included the capability of underwing mounted ordnance, missile capability and rocket pods. A few special versions could even carry a nuclear payload.

The Canberra first saw front line action in 1955 when 101 Squadron was sent to Malaya to stop terrorists. A couple of years later it was back in action again during the Suez Crisis and again in Egypt. By this time the Canberra had established itself as the bedrock of RAF Bomber Command, however with the Cold War gathering momentum and the perceived need for a growing strategic nuclear deterrent, the Canberra was quickly superseded by a new range of dedicated long-range heavy bombers. The introduction of the V-force (the Vulcan, Victor and Valiant) saw the Canberra retired from bombing services by 1961, but this was far from the end of the Canberra's RAF career. It would carry on as a high-level photo-reconnaissance aircraft for another thirty years, flying high-altitude observation missions in Northern Ireland, Bosnia, Kosovo, as well as Afghanistan in the early 2000s, some fifty years after the first Canberras entered service.

The success of the aircraft with the RAF meant that many other international air forces were interested including Australia, Argentina, India, France, Sweden, West Germany and the United States, who built the Canberra under licence and renaming it the Martin B-57. Including the B-57, approximately 1,400 aircraft were built, 773 of which saw service in the RAF.

Multi record breaker

On 31 August 1951, test pilot Roland Beamont set a new transatlantic record in a Canberra, crossing from Aldergrove, Northern Ireland to Gander, Newfoundland in 4hrs 18mins 29.4 seconds. On 26 August 1952, he repeated the trip and back again in 10hrs 3mins – the first one-day return crossing of the Atlantic. Canberras also broke the world altitude record three times.

English Electric Canberra B2 (RAF serial WD940) which
was used as the U.S. Air Force B-57 prototype in 1951

Crew:

3 🧍🧍🧍

Max Speed:

580

mph
(933 km/h)

Armament:

4 x 20mm Hispano
Mk.V cannons in
ventral gunpack

2 x 7.62mm machine
gun pods

2 x 37 x 51mm rocket pods
OR

2 x Matra 18 x SNEB 68mm
rocket pods

Up to 8000lb of internal
and external ordnance

Range:

810

miles (965km)

Service Ceiling:

49,213

feet (15,000m)

48 Hawker Hunter

Hawker Aircraft Ltd rose from the ashes of the Sopwith Aviation Company when Sopwith test pilot, Harry Hawker, along with three others (including Thomas Sopwith) bought the assets of the bankrupt Sopwith organisation and formed H.G. Hawker Engineering in 1920, renaming themselves Hawker Aircraft Ltd in 1933.

Not surprisingly, given this kind of history, many RAF squadrons in the run up to WW2 were full of Hawker designs such as the Fury, Demon and Hart. Then there was the Hurricane which, along with the Spitfire, spearheaded the defence of Britain in 1940.

After the war, the newly installed Labour government were convinced that no major conflict would take place anywhere that would concern Britain for at least a decade and therefore decided there would be no need to invest in any new aircraft until the mid-1950s at the earliest. However, with the emergence of the Cold War the RAF quickly realised they urgently needed a new range of fighters. The situation got so bad that in 1950 the RAF took the unprecedented step of ordering two fighter planes 'off the drawing board' without actually seeing or testing them. One of them was the Supermarine Swift, the other was the Hawker Hunter.

The first Hunter prototype took to the skies on 20 July 1951; ten months later a second prototype loaded with numerous improvements including gun provisions was put through its paces. Much thought had been put into making the Hunter a quality interceptor; it had power controls making it very easy to manoeuvre in the air. It was also agile on the ground with a single-point refuelling system and a self-contained gun 'cassette' that slotted directly into the nose of the aircraft ensuring that turnaround times in between sorties were kept to an absolute minimum. By 1954, the Hunter was beginning to appear in numbers within the RAF's front-line squadrons. Pilots loved them despite a few design flaws, not least a tiny fuel load.

The Hunter took part in many operations around the world during its time as a frontline fighter. They escorted Canberra bombers during the Suez Crisis in 1956, although their lack of range did limit their operational effectiveness. These planes were involved in the Brunei Revolt in 1962 and in Aden from 1964–1967 where they were engaged in a number of ground attacks. The Hunter stayed in active service with RAF until 1976, when it was finally replaced by the Hawker Harrier. Over the years 1,972 were manufactured with dozens of overseas air forces taking Hunters into their fleet, including Sweden, India, Jordan, Switzerland and Singapore.

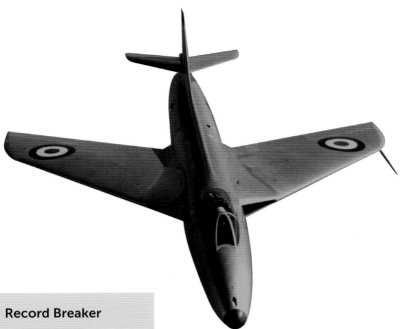

Record Breaker

On 7 September 1953, Neville Duke, decorated wartime fighter pilot and Hawker test pilot, broke the world speed record in a Hawker Hunter, reaching 727.63mph (1171kmh). The record stood for nineteen days until it was broken by a Supermarine Swift.

"It was the first fighter aircraft to have power controls which meant whatever speed you were flying it was very light on the controls... you could use just two fingers to do a roll."

Group Captain Chris Christie, former Hawker Hunter pilot

Crew:

1

Max Speed:

715
mph
(1,150 km/h)

Armament:

Four nose-mounted 30mm cannon

49 Hawker P.1127 Harrier

During the mid-1950s the engineering department of Bristol Engine Company were playing with ideas around the concept of vertical flight. In 1957 they called up the head engineer of Hawker, Sidney Camm, to tell him of their project, which was basically to use four separate rotating nozzles that could vary the angle of thrust from their engines and form stable 'legs' that would enable a plane to take off and land vertically.

Not surprisingly, Camm was interested and immediately put a team of men on the case to see what could be developed. The project had to be privately funded due to government budget cuts, but despite this the first prototype of the P.1127 was delivered for testing in July 1960, with its first tethered flight taking place on 21 October 1960. During that first test, Hawker test pilot, Bill Bedford, raised the aircraft a few feet off the ground in a tethered hover. A flying revolution had just begun.

A second prototype was built and over the next year or so stringent testing aimed to perfect the transition from hovering to forward flight and from forward flight back to hover to ensure a safe landing. As things progressed the idea of operating from an aircraft carrier was mutely trialled, with P.1127 executing the first vertical landing on a carrier (HMS *Ark Royal*) in 1963.

There were many issues with the prototypes, which was not surprising given what the engineers at Hawker were trying to achieve. The first three prototypes all crashed, but the development team persisted. Whilst the P.1127 had been strictly an experimental design, the Hawker Siddeley Kestrel, which incorporated some of the latest design improvements, became the developmental machine and first flew in March 1964. Nine were built in total and they were used to evaluate the performance and potential of the technology. Once the Kestrels had successfully completed their training, the first production machines started to take shape – these were now to be known as Harriers.

The RAF ordered sixty Harrier GR1 machines in 1966; three years later the first examples began to make their way to front line squadrons. It was deployed in numbers at Gütersloh near the East German border and became the RAF's main ground attack aircraft. If the Russians released their tanks across Europe, the Harrier would have been first in the queue to try and stop them in their tracks.

Over the next fifteen years the Harrier would be used for numerous different roles within the RAF including close air-support, reconnaissance and more conventional ground-attack missions. In 1982, the Harrier saw action in the

Falklands, operating from aircraft carriers along side Sea Harriers from the Royal Navy. During this conflict they provided critical air support for the British ground troops as well as being engaged directly in attacking enemy positions.

After the war, a shortage of money slowed development of the Harrier down to a crawl but a joint US/UK venture between McDonnel Douglas and British Aerospace conjured up the Harrier II, which entered service in the late 1980s as the GR5 with later upgrades leading to the GR7 and then the GR9. It became one of the most reliable and capable machines in the RAF's fleet, seeing action in Bosnia, Iraq and Afghanistan before being retired in 2011 after more than forty years service.

The first of its kind

The Harrier was the first of its kind with VTOL (Vertical Take Off and Landing) capability. Only in the summer of 2018 will the RAF have another Squadron capable of VTOL when 617 Squadron is fully equipped with the new F-35B Lightning.

Auctioned Harrier

A 1976 Hawker Siddeley Harrier GR3 Jump Jet 'in time capsule condition' was sold at auction in July 2014 for £105,800.

Queen's Commendation

On 30 October 1962 Hawker's deputy chief test pilot Hugh Merewether suffered a catastrophic engine failure and fire over West Sussex whilst flying a P.1127 prototype. Rather than eject, he managed a high-speed glide landing at RAF Tangmere thereby allowing engineers to investigate the cause. In recognition of this feat, Merewether was awarded the Queen's Commendation for Valuable Service in the Air.

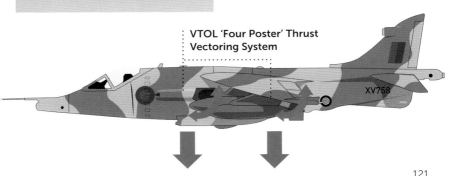

VTOL 'Four Poster' Thrust Vectoring System

XV758

50 V Force

After the end of WW2, RAF Bomber Command continued with its policy of using a massed formation of heavy bombers in large air raids against enemy positions. However, with the onset of the nuclear age there were many within the corridors of power at Bomber Command that thought this was a bit old fashioned. Why have hundreds of traditional bombers when one bomber armed with a nuclear bomb could wipe out an entire city on its own?

The arrival of the Cold War added to the pressure on the Air Ministry to revamp its bomber fleet and in January 1947 it issued a request for an advance jet-bomber that would be at least equal in performance and capability than anything the Americans or Russians had up their sleeves. In response to this request, British aircraft manufacturers Avro and Handley Page came up with some revolutionary designs (they would become the delta winged Vulcan and the crescent-winged Victor) – both were awarded contracts as insurance against the other failing. Vickers-Armstrong came up with a slightly more mainstream design (that would become the Valiant) and they were also given a contract as a further insurance policy against both radical designs failing.

The Valiant was the first V-bomber – they were called V-bombers or the V-force because all their given names started with the letter 'V' – to go into production and entered service in 1955. The Vulcan followed a year later with the Victor appearing in April 1958.

In their design, particular attention had been given to quick reaction times, speed and manoeuvrability – especially in the Vulcan which could start all four of its engines simultaneously with little ground support needed and take off from short runways. At 'readiness state' it could be in the air within fifteen minutes. The end result of this was that the V-force was capable of destroying targets hours before NATO bombers were in the air.

Throughout the early stages of the Cold War, NATO looked towards the RAF's V-force to threaten key cities in Russian territories. With all three V-bombers able to fly higher than any Russian interceptor, it was estimated that the V-force was capable of killing eight million Russians and wounding another eight million before American NATO forces had even entered Russian airspace.

All of the V-force saw active service at least once: the Valiant in the Suez Canal crisis of 1956, the Victor in the Indonesia-Malaysia conflict of 1962–66 and the Vulcan in the Falklands War. Additionally, during the Cuban Missile Crisis the V-force were put on fifteen minutes' notice.

Over time, the development of anti-aircraft missiles meant the V-force threat became increasingly ineffective and in 1963 the decision was to change their roles, first to that of low-level bombers, and then as air-to-air refuelling tankers. The Valiant was retired from RAF service first in 1965, and after the Falklands the Vulcan's days as a bomber were over although a few tanker versions continued to operate until 1984. Victor tankers served operationally until 1993.

15 minutes readiness

On 1 February 1962, V-force started its Quick Reaction Alert readiness commitment of one loaded weapon system and crew per operational squadron at constant standby with a fifteen-minute readiness window – an arrangement that continued until 30 June 1969.

The first British Hydrogen bomb

A Vickers Valiant of No. 49 Squadron dropped the first British hydrogen bomb (Yellow Sun) near Christmas Island on 15 May 1957.

Avro Vulcan B Mk2

Crew: 5
Max Speed: 646mph (1,040kmh)
Range: 4,598 miles (7400km)
Service Ceiling: 55,000ft (16,764m)
Bombload: 21,000lb
Total Production: 136

Handley Page Victor B. Mk2

Crew: 5
Max Speed: 640mph (1,030kmh)
Range: 4,598 miles (7.400 km)
Service Ceiling: 52,493ft (16,000m)
Bombload: 35,000lb
Total Production: 86

Vickers Valiant B Mk 1

Crew: 5
Max Speed: 414mph (666kmh)
Range: 4,474miles (7,200km)
Service Ceiling: 68,898ft (21,000m)
Bombload: 21,000lb
Total Production: 107

51 TSR-2

With the advent of increasingly sophisticated Russian radar-guided surface-to-air missiles in the 1950s it was becoming very obvious to anyone who cared to look that it was increasingly difficult to guarantee a plane's safety whilst out on manoeuvres, even if flying at very high altitude.

The RAF needed a replacement for the old Canberra bomber but as they spelt out their 'wants list' for a new machine it became clear that whatever was designed and built would be a very special machine indeed. It would need to be able to fly at Mach 2 at high altitude and hit Mach 1 at low level (below 1,000ft /305m) – regardless of weather conditions. It would also need to be able to carry out detailed photo-reconnaissance missions at high speed from various altitudes day or night, carry a tactical nuclear weapon over 1,000 nautical miles (1850km) and take off from short runways. Whichever way you looked at it, it was a huge technological challenge for the time.

Following some political shenanigans, the contract was finally awarded to a consortium of three companies – English Electric and long-time competitors Vickers-Armstrongs, along with engine maker Bristol who begrudgingly joined forces to form the British Aircraft Corporation and set to work designing the TSR-2 (Tactical Strike and Reconnaissance, Mach 2).

What they came up with was one of the most aerodynamically advanced designs of the time, with angled wing-tips and a narrow fuselage containing cockpit, fuel, engines and weapons. There was also a ground-breaking navigation/attack digital computer system and hugely powerful Bristol turbojet engines which had the potential to force a renaming of the TSR-2 to TSR-3.

On 27 September 1964 the first test flight was made on Boscombe Down. That first flight lasted just fifteen minutes and took place with the undercarriage down and the engine power strictly controlled. By the end of March 1965, the aircraft had completed twenty-four test flights, most concerned with the basic flying qualities of the aircraft which, according to the test pilots involved, were outstanding. However, costs continued to rise and the TSR-2 was still falling short in many of the initial requirements laid out by the Air Ministry, such as take off distance and combat radius.

During cabinet meetings on 1 April 1965 it was decided to cancel the TSR-2 project on the grounds of cost and instead put in an order to purchase F-111 fighters from the USA after being offered a better price and delivery dates from US manufacturer General Dynamics. Therefore, the TSR-2 must go down in history as the greatest aircraft the RAF never had.

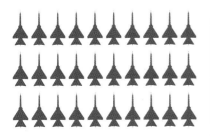

Dennis Healey estimated the cost in 1967 to be

£1,700m

over fifteen years — equating to £56 million per aircraft
(based on an order of thirty)

"The trouble with the TSR-2 was that it tried to combine the most advanced state of every art in every field. The aircraft firms and the RAF were trying to get the Government on the hook and understated the cost. But TSR-2 cost far more than even their private estimates, and so I have no doubt about the decision to cancel."

Denis Healey, then
Minister of Defence

Crew:

2 👥

Max Speed:

Mach
2.35

Armament:

Total weapons load of 10,000lb (4,500kg)

Range:

2,780
miles (4,470 km)
at Mach 0.92

1,000
miles (1,600km)
at Mach 2

Service Ceiling:

40,000
feet (12,000m)

52 McDonnell Douglas F4 Phantom

Originally it was the Royal Navy who ordered the first batch of McDonnell Douglas F4 Phantom aircraft. In 1964 they signed up for 143 machines with the idea that they would be used on their soon-to-be-expanded aircraft carrier fleet to work a dual role of air defence and strike attack. Unfortunately for the Royal Navy, in 1966 the Government decided to cancel the two new aircraft carriers which led to the Phantom order being cut right back to just fifty machines.

Another naval cancellation – this time the planned refit of HMS *Eagle* that would have allowed her to operate the Phantom – meant that twenty of the fifty aircraft on order were given to the RAF in an effort to back up its fleet of English Electric Lightning interceptors. The Lightning was struggling with combat range and weaponry, especially for long interception missions in the north against Russia. To help out, on 1 September 1969, a new Phantom squadron was put together at RAF Leuchars, the UK's most northerly air defence base at that time.

Over the following few years several new Phantom squadrons were formed, especially in Germany. However, with the introduction of the SEPECAT Jaguar as a ground attack and reconnaissance aircraft, a large number of the German-based Phantoms were recalled to the UK between 1974–1977 to undertake UK air defence roles with the Jaguar

being stationed in larger numbers at the German frontier.

In May 1982, three Phantoms from 29 Squadron were deployed at RAF Ascension Island to provide air cover during the Falklands War, but they struggled with covering the huge distances and were largely ineffective. In August of that year, after the end of the conflict, 29 Squadron moved to RAF Stanley to provide local air cover for the Islands, soon to be replaced by 23 Squadron who were to stay there until 1988. To backfill the hole left by 23 Squadron leaving the UK defence network, the RAF purchased fifteen Phantoms from the US Navy.

The end of the Cold War saw a gradual reduction in the number of active and operational Phantom squadrons and despite a brief reprieve during the First Gulf War by 1991 the UK Phantom force had been reduced to four squadrons, all based at RAF Wattisham. The end of an era was marked on 1 October 1992, when 74 Squadron, the final remaining Phantom squadron of the RAF, performed a farewell formation flypast.

There would be one final twist in the UK Phantom story and it is not a happy ending. Ludicrously, despite being partly manufactured by UK firms and bought with UK taxpayer's money, the USA had stipulated that the aircraft could not be disposed of to non-government organisations. As a result an important part of the UK's aviation history has for the most part been reduced to scrap despite museums across the country crying out for a chance to exhibit an example of this powerful aircraft. A few have somehow escaped this madness from above, but it is a small number.

JAG Killer

On 25 May 1982, a SEPECAT Jaguar GR.1 XX963 flown by Steve Griggs was shot down in a 'friendly fire' incident by an RAF Phantom, with Griggs having to eject to safety as his Jaguar crashed into farmland approximately 35 miles from RAF Bruggen in West Germany.

The crew of the Phantom would eventually stand before a court martial. In the spirit of the RAF's macabre sense of humour the Phantom involved, Phantom FGR.2 XV422, received nose art depicting a Jaguar GR.1 silhouette with the title 'Jag Killer' underneath which the aircraft wore until it was scrapped in 1998.

David Gowans / Alamy

One of the most famous Phantoms to see RAF service, XV582 (nicknamed Black Mike because of its paintwork) was the first FG.1 machine to pass 5,000 flying hours. She was also used in the record breaking 'Lands End to John O'Groats Run' on 1 April 1989, where she covered the 590 mile distance in just 46 minutes and 44 seconds – an average speed of over 757 mph.

Crew:

2

Max Speed:

1,386
mph
(2,231 km/h)

Range:

1,750
miles (2820km)

Service Ceiling:

57,200
feet (17,400m)

Armament:

4 × AIM-7 Sparrow or Skyflash in fuselage recesses

4 × AIM-9 Sidewinders on wing pylons

1 × 20 mm (0.787 in) M61 Vulcan 6-barrel Gatling cannon in SUU-23 gun pod

Up to 180 SNEB 68mm unguided rockets

11 × 1000lb free fall or retarded bombs

53 Boeing CH-47 Chinook

The Boeing Chinook is a tandem-rotor helicopter that first entered service with the US Army on 16 August 1962. Just a few years later it was thrown into the deep end in Vietnam where it proved itself an excellent workhorse, especially as a heavy lifting machine. The lack of a tail rotor means that almost one hundred per cent of its power can be used for lifting, making it ideal for salvaging and aircraft recovery missions. During the Vietnam war the Chinook returned thousands of disabled aircraft which could then be recycled, saving the US government billions of dollars. The Chinook CH-47A was an immediate success.

The Chinook didn't enter RAF service until 1980, despite an initial order placed in 1968 which was subsequently cancelled following heavy lobbying from UK manufacturers. The first fleet of thirty-three machines were CH-47C models which had significant performance upgrades over the original version. In 1982, four Chinooks were loaded up onto the container ship SS *Atlantic Conveyor* bound for the Falklands. That ship was hit by an Argentinian Exocet missile, destroying the ship and its cargo. Luckily for one Chinook (Bravo November) it was on a training flight at the time of the attack and managed to land on HMS *Hermes* and proceeded to work as the only serviceable heavy lift helicopter available to British forces during the war. In addition to the Falklands campaign, RAF Chinooks have also seen extended

service in the Balkans, Northern Ireland, Iraq and Afghanistan. During the latter campaigns CH-47s took up an invaluable emergency response role and sometimes became a mobile hospital. In many ways the Chinook became the defining image of the UK's presence and commitment in Afghanistan.

The most recent variant of the Chinook is the CH-47F. Boasting a modernised airframe, the latest in avionic technology, three gun positions and a reconfigured and customisable cabin, the latest version of this timeless machine is hugely versatile and will continue to be a real asset to the RAF for years to come.

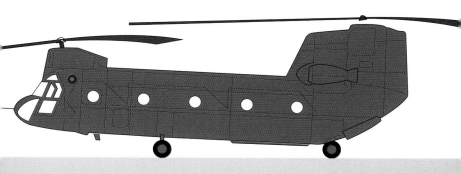

Crew:

2 pilots

1 loadmaster

1 crewman

Max Speed:

302 mph **(486 km/h)**

The RAF Chinook fleet is the largest fleet outside of the USA

Range:

200 miles **(370.4km)**

Service Ceiling:

20,000 feet **(6,069m)**

54 Bravo November

Chinook HC2 ZA718/BN, otherwise known as *Bravo November*, has a remarkable story and, outside of the Battle of Britain Memorial Flight, is potentially the most significant machine still flying in the RAF's possession. With four Distinguished Flying Crosses (DFC) to its name, ZA718 has seen action all around the globe and has a service record second to none. In the past twenty-eight years it has served in the Falkland Islands, Lebanon, Germany, Northern Ireland, Kurdistan, Iraq and Afghanistan. That's an impressive list by any stretch of the imagination.

The story of *Bravo November* begins in April 1982 when it was wrapped in plastic and loaded aboard the container ship *Atlantic Conveyor* along with three other Chinooks. These four machines, along with six Wessex helicopters and tonnes of supplies were all bound for the Falklands. On 25 May the *Atlantic Conveyor* was due to sail into San Carlos to offload its cargo when it was struck by an Argentinian Exocet missile and destroyed with the loss of twelve members of the crew. Luckily *Bravo November* was airborne on a test flight at the time of the attack and the crew managed to make it to the safety of the aircraft carrier HMS *Hermes*.

Despite having no spares, tools or lubricants, as they were all lost in the attack, *Bravo November* was immediately put to use moving ammunition up to frontline artillery batteries and then carrying 105mm howitzer guns to support SAS troops on Mount Kent whilst were under direct fire from Argentinian artillery.

On a later mission, it ran into a snowstorm on its way back to San Carlos Water. The altimeter failed, and the helicopter crashed into the sea at 100 knots. The impact threw up spray that flooded the engine intakes but pilot Squadron Leader Dick Langworthy and his co-pilot Flight Lieutenant Andy Lawless managed to get the helicopter back in the air and eventually to safety despite damage to the fuselage, and with no navigation or communication systems and no pilot's door which had been ripped off on impact with the water.

On 2 June, eighty-one paratroopers were squeezed into ZA718 as they were flown from Goose Green to Fitzroy to seize the settlement, this was almost double the maximum payload and still stands as a record for a troop-carrying helicopter anywhere in the world. By the time the Argentinians surrendered, *Bravo November* had flown for 109 hours and carried 1,500 troops, 95 casualties, 550 prisoners of war and 550 tons of cargo. Squadron Leader Langworthy was awarded a DFC for his bravery.

Twenty years after the Falklands campaign *Bravo November* was on its way to the Middle East on board HMS *Ark Royal* in the build up to the invasion of Iraq.

Chinook HC2 ZA718/BN

During Operation 'Telic', *Bravo November* spearheaded the assault on the Al Faw peninsula, the site of a major oil refinery, and was the first British helicopter to land Royal Marines ashore. During a three-day period, the aircraft averaged nineteen flight-hours per day, delivering combat vehicles, artillery and troops. It was the largest helicopter mission the RAF had ever undertaken and Squadron Leader Steve Carr, the pilot of *Bravo November*, was awarded the DFC for his role in the operation.

Three years later, on the night of 11 June 2006, Flight Lieutenant Craig Wilson was captain of *Bravo November* in Helmand when he was ordered to recover a casualty from a landing site. Even though he had done little night flying in the country, he flew at 150 feet, made a precision landing and recovered the casualty. A few hours later he was back on another evacuation mission, although this time he was forced to delay his landing while an Apache gunship suppressed enemy fire.

After this, despite having been on duty for twenty-two hours, Flight Lieutenant Wilson volunteered to deliver reinforcements to threatened troops. He also brought back two wounded soldiers, saving their lives. His actions earned him the DFC – *Bravo November's* third.

In 2010, *Bravo November* was involved in another DFC-winning incident while on service in Afghanistan piloted by Flight Lieutenant Ian Fortune. The machine was fired at by Taliban fighters during an attempted rescue of wounded soldiers. As Fortune attempted to take off an enemy round was fired through the windshield hitting the front of Fortune's helmet, smashing his visor and severely lacerating his face. Despite all this and despite the Chinook taking further hits that damaged its stability systems, Fortune managed to get the Chinook safely back to Camp Bastion and all casualties survived.

There is a *Bravo November* exhibit at the RAF Museum in London.

ZA718 Bravo November, releases decoy flares.

> **"Bravo November is a hugely significant aeroplane to the RAF, the RAF almost never singles out individual aircraft for tribute. But Bravo November is exceptional."**

Retired Air Chief Marshal Sir Richard Johns

55 Typhoon FGR4

Developed by the UK, Germany, Italy and Spain the first orders for the Eurofighter Typhoon FGR4 were placed in 1998. Fifty-three aircraft were ordered initially and deliveries started to filter through to 17(R) Squadron RAF in 2003. Two years later the first Typhoon Squadron formed at RAF Coningsby in Lincolnshire and on 29 July 2007 the Typhoon took over the UK's air defence.

Those initial aircraft only had air-to-air capability, however, there was a growing requirement for air-to-ground capability and by the summer of 2008 a new and improved version of the Eurofighter was declared combat-ready in an air-to-ground role too.

With two Eurojet EJ200 engines the Typhoon can hit Mach 1.8 and fly up to 55,000ft. With its flexible armament capability, the Typhoon can carry out a wide variety of missions ranging from simple patrolling of airspace to full on dog-fighting. On April 2011, a mixed pair of RAF Typhoon and Tornado GR4[207] dropped precision-guided bombs on ground vehicles operated by Gaddafi forces that were parked in an abandoned tank park in Libya.

Designed to help the pilot and aircraft communicate efficiently, the Eurofighter has a highly automated cockpit that gives the pilot the right information at the right time. The way the cockpit is designed is no accident, representing detailed consideration of all the human factors. The aircraft responds to voice, throttle and stick commands that are instant and instinctive. Thanks to this, and coupled with the Eurofighter's carefree handling, the flying element is relatively straightforward.

The first batch of Eurofighters that were delivered in 2003 are currently in the process of being retired, with another forty on order to replace them, leaving the RAF with 107 Typhoon aircraft in service until 2030.

3(F) Squadron RAF Eurofighter Typhoon based at RAF Coningsby, Lincoln, England firing an ASRAAM missile

The Eurofighter
Typhoon is fitted
with two Eurojet
EJ200 engines

Engine Performance

It takes about 1 minute 30
seconds after take-off to reach
more than 30,000 feet, all the
while maintaining intercept
airspeed.

The aircraft's supercruise
capability gives the Eurofighter
the ability to intercept possible
targets with supersonic speed,
without the need to use reheat
abilities (its afterburner), which
optimizes fuel consumption.

Start Up

The automated engine start-up,
combined with several dedicated
QRA-modes (Quick Reaction
Alert)for the navigation system,
allows for an extremely short time
frame from scramble to wheels off
the ground.

The auxiliary power unit can be
started by ground crew while the
pilot is entering the cockpit after
scramble, again gaining precious
time.

Crew:

1

Max Speed:

1,550
mph
(2,495 kmh at 10,975m altitude)

Armament:

Paveway IV,
AMRAAM,
ASRAAM,
Mauser 27mm
Cannon,
Enhanced
Paveway II,
Brimstone

Range:

1,750
miles (2820km)

Service Ceiling:

55,000
feet (16,765m)

56 General Atomics MQ-9 Reaper

The idea of a pilotless drone aircraft is not a new one. During WW2 the Germans had the V1 and the Americans played with the 'Aphrodite' programme of using radio controlled B-17 bombers. The MQ-9 Reaper is a remote piloted aircraft designed for Intelligence, Surveillance and Reconnaissance (ISR) but one that can turn its hand to ground attack should its remote pilot-commander so wish. With eight hard points under the wings it can carry an assortment of weaponry up to a maximum payload of 4,200lb (1,905kg) such as Hellfire air-to-surface missiles and laser guided bombs.

Designed and built in America, the RAF's fleet of MQ-9 Reaper drones were first deployed to Afghanistan in 2007. In total, ten RAF Reapers flew over 50,000 flight hours in Afghanistan, gathering vital intelligence as well as dropping several hundred guided weapons. Launched from an airfield within or close to the combat zone, the operational missions were flown by pilots positioned in local ground control stations aided by additional mission controllers based at Creech Air Force Base in the USA. This was achieved by using advanced satellite technology to operate the drone beyond the horizon. Once the mission was complete the control of the drone was handed back to the local ground control team for landing.

During 2013, the RAF moved Reaper operations from the USA to the UK, with 13 Squadron at RAF Waddington becoming the first UK-based Reaper unit. Since October 2014, several Reaper drones from this fleet have been in action against the Islamic State group providing surveillance and situational analysis for coalition forces on the ground.

These live missions go to show the important role drones already have within the RAF and there is no doubt such pilotless machines will have a lot to say in the future as the RAF begins its next one hundred years.

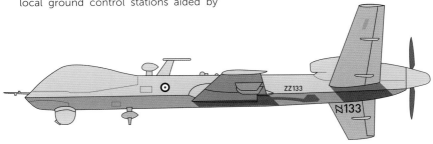

A Reaper, part of 39 Squadron Royal Air Force. Medium-to-high altitude, long endurance Remotely Piloted Air System (RPAS). The Reaper's primary mission is to act as an Intelligence, Surveillance and Reconnaissance (ISR) asset, employing sensors to provide real-time data to commanders and intelligence specialists

Crew:

0 onboard

2 🚶🚶
at ground station

Max Speed:

300
mph
(482 km/h)

Range:

1,151
miles (1,852km)

Service Ceiling:

50,000
feet (15,000m)

Fighting
Moments

57 The First Battle of Britain

The first successful aerial attack on Britain took place on Christmas Eve 1914 when a German aircraft dropped a single bomb on the port of Dover. The device was probably intended for Dover Castle which was being used as a military base at the time, but it missed its target and ended up blowing a ten-foot crater in a local garden.

It was an inauspicious start to what would be a series of intermittent air attacks from Germany that would steadily increase in intensity before petering out in mid-1918. In total, 9,000 bombs were dropped on Britain during WW1, killing 1,412 and seriously injuring 3,408 more.

Initially these raids were carried out by a small number of aircraft that could only drop a limited number of bombs, but on the night of 19 January 1915 the Germans sent over Zeppelins to carry out a bombing raid. These giant airships were up to 600ft long and capable of carrying two tonnes of bombs — they were an altogether different proposition.

Despite their huge size these airships were not easy to spot, especially at night and even harder to bring down. In 1915, Britain's anti-aircraft defence system was limited to just a few emplacements around key areas of the South of England, and the handful of planes operated by RFC home defence squadrons didn't have any armament at all. Crew had to rely on their own pistols which was a complete waste of time. Even machine-guns were ineffective, with the bullets passing right through and failing to ignite the hydrogen gas of the airship.

Something needed to be done to improve the situation. During 1916, banks of searchlights and anti-aircraft guns were organised in a much more effective way to cover more of the country. Incendiary and explosive ammunition made a big impact and in September 1916 Lieutenant William Leefe Robinson brought down the first German Airship on British soil using these new bullets. He won the Victoria Cross and became something of a national hero in the process.

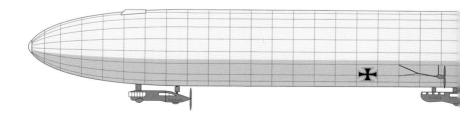

By the end of the war, London alone was defended by 304 guns, 415 searchlights and eleven fighter squadrons. The raids by the Zeppelins and later the huge Gotha bombers, taught the Royal Flying Corps, and later the RAF, huge lessons in how to organise air defence systems – something they would put into great effect in 1940 when Britain was once again under attack from the air.

51
air raids by German airships

52
air raids by German aircraft

Over 9,000

bombs were dropped on to British targets

"There was a terrific explosion and my mother said 'Quick we're being shelled. Go down to the cellar.' This was because a destroyer had put a few shells into Hartlepool on the north-east coast of Britain a few days before.

We didn't then know that it was possible for an aeroplane to come over and drop bombs in anger."

Mr Youden. Eyewitness to the Dover bombing on 24 December 1914

Legendary cricketer W.G. Grace would often stand outside his London home shaking his fist and shouting at German Zeppelins as they circled London. During one raid in 1915 he collapsed from a stroke and died a few days later.

People injured:
3,408

People killed:
1,412

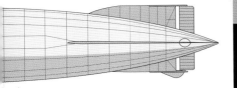

First World War
Graf Zeppelin

Three times as many people from outside of London were killed during the German raids

58 The Battle of Britain

On 16 July 1940, less than a month after the fall of France, Adolf Hitler issued Führer Directive No.16:

> 'Since England, in spite of her hopeless military situation, shows no signs of being ready to come to an understanding, I have decided to prepare a landing operation against England and, if necessary to carry it out.'

The operation was codenamed *Seelowe* (Sealion). A few weeks later Hitler issued Führer Directive No. 17: 'For the conduct of air and sea warfare against England'. He knew that the Luftwaffe needed to be master of the English skies if *Seelowe* was to stand any chance of success. The air attack on England would be codenamed *Adlerangriff* (Attack of the Eagle) and would officially start on *Adlertag* (Eagle Day) although the exact day would be determined by the weather. Large scale air attacks over Britain began in earnest on 10 July 1940: Sixty Junkers JU-88 fighter bombers smashed targets at Falmouth, Swansea and Ipswich. Meanwhile twenty-five Dornier Do-17 bombers attacked a convoy of ships in the Dover Straits.

The Battle in numbers:

The RAF initially deployed

1,300

Fighter command pilots

= 100 pilots/ aircraft

The Luftwaffe deployed 4,000 pilots

Luftwaffe aircraft at start of the battle:

1,700 Bombers

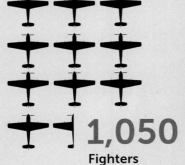

1,050
Fighters

RAF aircraft at start of the battle:

650
Fighters

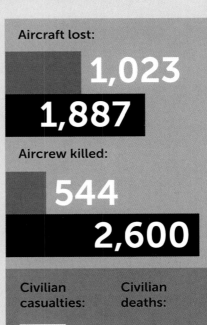

Aircraft lost:

1,023

1,887

Aircrew killed:

544

2,600

Civilian casualties:

Civilian deaths:

90,000

40,000

2,936
pilots flew at least one operational sortie with the R.A.F. between 10th July and 31st October 1940

595
pilots from other allied countries fought in the battle.

544
fighter pilots killed

20
average age of an RAF pilot in 1940

£264
average pilot officer salary, equivalent to £30,000 today.

15
the number of other nations whose pilots flew with Britain in the battle.

18th August - The Hardest Day

The Luftwaffe launches three huge attacks in a last-ditch effort to destroy Fighter Command

Sorties flown: 927 970

Aircraft lost: 68 69

After the 18th August the weather deteriorated and the intensity of the fighting dropped significantly. Back in Germany, Hitler postponed Operation *Sealion* indefinitely whilst Hermann Goering, the head of the Luftwaffe, decided to change his tactics from attacking Fighter Command directly to the strategic bombing of military targets. The Battle of Britain was over, the Luftwaffe had failed to take control of British skies.

"I went straight at them and when I was 2,000 yards away I started firing and I didn't stop. At the last second, I dived underneath the leading German plane, still firing. One of them put a bullet into my engine. The fuel was pouring out."

Pilot Officer John Ellacombe DFC & Bar.
Hurricane Pilot during the Battle of Britain

60 A day in the life of a Battle of Britain Pilot

For sixteen hours a day, every day for sixteen weeks in 1940, the pilots of Fighter Command were in a constant state of readiness to meet the enemy head-on. Here is what a typical day would have looked like.

Woken at dawn

04:00

All fighter pilots were awake at dawn. A cup of tea started their day, often made for them by a junior member of the ground crew. They wash and dress before being driven to the dispersal area next to the runway. Here they will have breakfast – if they have time – and wait for the alarm.

SCRAMBLE!

10:00

By mid-morning the radar stations along the coast of England start picking up signals from incoming enemy aircraft. The dispersal phone rings and is answered by the duty officer. Once he has all the information he will switch on the tannoy system and shout 'Scramble!' into the receiver where it is heard across the airfield.

Into the air

10:07

Having raced to their planes, attached their parachutes and clambered aboard their aircraft (which are already running, courtesy of ground crew) the pilots begin to taxi down the runway and take to the air.

Mission briefing

10:10

In the rush to get airborne there is no time for a briefing. Once safely in the air they would receive instructions through their headphones. 'Vector two three zero, bandits 100 plus, Angels two zero' which was code for them to steer a course for 230 degrees where more than 100 enemy aircraft are approaching at approximately 20,000 feet.

Engage enemy

10:15

The briefing was accurate and very soon enemy planes are spotted heading in from the east with the sun at their back. A huge dogfight begins with RAF fighter pilots duelling with German fighters or attacking slower moving bombers.

The fight is over

10:40

Luftwaffe fighter pilots can only fight over England for a limited period of time before they start to run out of fuel and are forced back to their bases in occupied Europe. RAF pilots will either return to base themselves or chase them back across the Channel, picking off any damaged enemy planes.

Return to base

11.00

Those pilots that survived the dogfight now all return to base. After landing they are interviewed by an Intelligence Officer who then compiles detailed combat reports covering all aspects of the fight including any enemy and RAF planes that have been shot down or damaged.

SCRAMBLE!

14.00

The second 'Scramble!' order of the day rings out over the tannoy system. This time the instructions suggest there are even more enemy aircraft heading their way. 'Vector one four five, bandits 200 plus, Angels three zero.' At the height of the battle, pilots would see combat two or three times a day.

Dismissed after dark

20.00

After sixteen hours of heightened anticipation and adrenaline filled violence in the air, the pilots are stood down as it begins to get dark. Those who have survived the day end it with dinner and a few pints of beer at the local pub. But not too many, as they will be up at 04:00 tomorrow morning to do it all again.

61 **Saving Buckingham Palace**

Ray Holmes joined the Royal Air Force Volunteer Reserve almost as soon as it had been launched. In fact he was the fifty-fifth person to sign on the dotted line; he joined as an airman pilot and was trained at Prestwick and Barton in Lancashire.

As the Battle of Britain began Holmes was already an experienced Hurricane pilot with 504 Squadron based out of RAF Hendon. At about midday on 15 September 1940, 504 Squadron were scrambled to intercept an incoming enemy raid that was heading straight for central London.

One of the German bombers, a Dornier Do 17, suffered engine problems on the approach to London and fell behind the main pack – it came under attack over Battersea from Hurricanes from 310 (Czech) Squadron and two of the crew bailed out. Despite the damage, the Dornier carried on deeper into London and was approaching Buckingham Palace (which had been targeted in the same raid) when Sergeant Holmes appeared on the scene.

In a last-ditch attempt to destroy the enemy plane, Holmes decided to ram it with his Hurricane. With a closing speed well in excess of 400mph, the result was devastating – the wing of the Hurricane sliced through the rear fuselage of the Dornier, detaching it completely, resulting in the enemy bomber crashing to the ground on the forecourt of Victoria Station.

Unfortunately, but not surprisingly, Holmes' Hurricane also received catastrophic damage and fell into a near vertical dive. Holmes managed to parachute to safety whilst his Hurricane smashed into the busy crossroads on Buckingham Palace Road at about 400mph. The impact punched a huge hole in the road which swallowed up most of the plane. After a safe landing Holmes managed to walk to the crash site, which by the time he got there was a huge water-filled crater with some wreckage scattered around the edges. After collecting a souvenir – a small piece of the Rolls-Royce Merlin's rocker cover with the letters 'S-R' of ROLLS-ROYCE – he was led to a local pub by some of the public that had gathered at the scene and bought drinks, before returning to Chelsea Barracks for a quick medical examination and then sent off back to Hendon.

The incident captured the imagination of the public – mainly because the enemy plane crashed in such a public place – with no loss of public life. It also helped that the incident was filmed too. Holmes was hailed as the RAF pilot who had saved Buckingham Palace by ramming an enemy bomber in mid-air. He continued to fly throughout the war, helped train Russian pilots on the

Hurricane, flew modified Spitfires on high altitude photo-reconnaissance missions and ended the war as the King's Messenger for the Prime Minister.

In 2004, the remains of his Hurricane were excavated and Holmes was once more reunited with his old aircraft. On close examination it was found that the firing button was set to FIRE. The aircraft's engine was recovered and put on display at the Imperial War Museum.

Some of the damage resulting from the collision caused loss of control in Holmes's Hurricane

"There was no time to weigh up the situation. His aeroplane looked so flimsy, I didn't think of it as solid and substantial. I just went on and hit it for six. I thought my aircraft would cut right through it, not allowing for the fact that his 'plane was as strong as mine!"

Sergeant Ray Holmes, 504 Squadron RAF

A still taken from film of the German Dornier Bomber, minus tail and wing tips, a second or so before it impacted Victoria Station

62 The Dambusters Raid

Pre-war intelligence had suggested to senior air staff leaders that the Ruhr Valley – the industrial heartland of Germany – consumed almost one third of all water in the country, and that the bulk of this water was contained in a vast reservoir contained by a single large dam known as the Möhne Dam. Along with the Möhne there were four or five other reservoirs in the immediate vicinity which fed inland waterways. It was agreed in 1938 that the destruction of these reservoirs would have serious consequences to German industry as well as her inland waterway system.

The matter of the dams was put on the back burner as war broke out, however, the basis of Operation *Chastise* had already been established:

1. **The destruction of the Möhne Dam would remove a large amount of the water needed for the industrial area of the Ruhr to continue to produce war materials;**

2. **The destruction of the smaller dams in the area would cause great disruption to a large proportion of Germany's inland waterways, upon which a great proportion of German industry relied;**

3. **The destruction of these dams would cause substantial damage to the surrounding infrastructure which would take time and resources to fix.**

Meanwhile, Barnes Wallis, an assistant chief designer at the Vickers-Armstrong Aviation section at Weybridge, Surrey, had been working on some ideas to breach the Ruhr dams. He had come up with a uniquely designed bomb that when dropped at a low enough altitude would actually skip over the water for a significant distance before smashing into the wall of the dam. After many trials and practice drops, the RAF gave the green light to modify a small number of Lancaster bombers in order to carry and drop the bomb in a live operation against the Ruhr dams.

The raids against the dams were given the codename Operation *Chastise* and took place on during the night of 16/17 May 1943 by 617 Squadron, RAF. Three waves of modified Lancaster bombers took off – formation No. 1 was made up of nine aircraft with the mission of attacking the Möhne Dam and then moving on to attack the Eder. Formation No. 2 numbered five aircraft and was to attack the Sorpe Dam and the third formation was to act as a mobile reserve either to attack the main dams if there were problems with the other two formations, or to attack some of the smaller dams in the area.

Formation No. 1 successfully breached both the Möhne and Eder Dams, however only one bomber out of formation No. 2 arrived safely at its target and was ultimately unable to breach the Sorpe Dam. Two bombers from the third formation attacked the Sorpe and Ennepe Dams but neither was breached. Eight of the original nineteen Lancasters that took off to destroy the Ruhr dams failed to return home.

Initial German casualty estimates from the floods when the dams broke were 1,294 killed, which included 749 French, Belgian, Dutch and Ukrainian prisoners of war. Later estimates put the death toll in the Möhne Valley at closer to 1,600, including people who drowned in the flood wave downstream from the dam.

617 Sqn Dam Busters Guy Gibson and crew of Lancaster BIII Special 'G' set out, May 1943

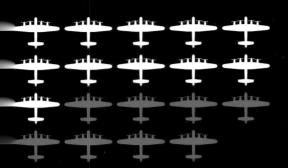

19

specially modified
Lancaster bombers
took part in the raid

● returned
● shot down

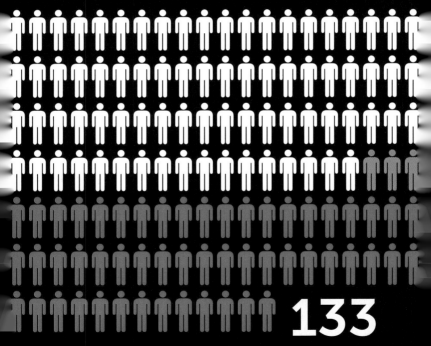

returned   killed   taken prisoner

133

aircrew flew in the
raid, 53 were killed

"I have to say the greatest satisfaction was on the way back... our route took us back over what had been the Möhne dam. There was water everywhere. It was just like an inland sea."

George "Johnny" Johnson - bomb aimer in Lancaster AJ-T, which attacked the Sorpe Dam on the night of 16/17 May 1943

The Bomb weighed 9250lb (4195KG) of which 6,600lb (2994KG) was the main explosive charge.

The Dambusters were awarded

37

medals for gallantry

1 x VC (Guy Gibson)
6 x DSO
10 x DFC
6 x Bars to the DFC
11 x DFM
1 x Bar to the DFM
2 x CGM (Flying)

The Lancaster had to drop the bomb 400-450 yards (400m) from the target at a height of just 60ft (18m) above the water, while maintaining a steady speed of 220mph (350kmh)

2 dams were breached

Searchlights and anti-aircraft guns

Torpedo nets

63 Thousand Bomber Raid

It had long been the view of many senior RAF officials that large-scale bombing raids had the potential to win a war without the need to rely on costly land battles. It was presumed that by bombing and destroying a country's industrial and manufacturing capacity it would quickly affect that country's material ability to wage war as well as significantly demoralising the public. However, when Arthur 'Bomber' Harris took over the reins of Bomber Command in February 1942 he knew that this particular arm of the RAF had yet to prove its worth.

The bombing campaigns of 1941 had not impacted the German war machine as had been hoped – mainly due to a lack of heavy bombers and poor bombing accuracy – it is estimated that only three per cent of all bombs dropped at this time landed within five miles of their target. The British public were getting restless and Harris knew it. He quickly proclaimed a new dawn for Bomber Command and with new tactics and, more importantly, new bombers, he was determined to make a success of the whole operation.

One of his big ideas was a series of 'Thousand Bomber Raids'.

A night-bombing raid consisting of 1,000 planes was incredibly ambitious on a number of levels, not least since Harris only had 400 operational bombers fit

and ready to fly. Training schools and reserve squadrons up and down the country were pillaged for any kind of plane that could fly to Germany and drop a bomb or two. The plan was to fly the bombers in a 'stream' formation in which all planes flew close together at the same speed on the same route to the target, thus overwhelming local defences with sheer weight of numbers. The planes at the front of the stream would drop flares and incendiaries to start fires and illuminate the target while the bombers that followed simply dropped their bombs onto the area that was burning. Theoretically this would result in more accurate bombing.

Initially the target for the first Thousand Bomber Raid was to be Hamburg, an important port and German naval centre, and thus a legitimate military target. However, adverse weather meant the attack on Hamburg couldn't happen. Cologne was chosen instead – it was Germany's third largest city but not an industrial power-house. The raid would now be a civilian terror raid rather than a strategic military one.

On 30 May 1942, 1,047 bombers of all shapes and sizes, along with a hundred or so other aircraft (there to occupy enemy fighters) took to the skies all over England. The raid allowed just ninety minutes for all bombers to pass over the city and release their bombs. In the end, approximately

1,500 tonnes of explosives were dropped on Cologne that night – two-thirds of these were incendiary bombs.

The damage caused was unprecedented. Twelve thousand non-residential buildings were damaged or destroyed including nine hospitals. Only one military building – an anti-aircraft barracks – was destroyed. On top of this, 13,000 homes were destroyed with another 28,000 damaged. Around 500 people were killed, over 5,000 people were injured and more than 45,000 people saw their homes go up in smoke.

With only four per cent losses, the first Thousand Bomber Raid was deemed a runaway success.

Forty-eight hours later, another huge raid targeted the Ruhr city of Essen. It was dubbed the Second Thousand Bomber Raid, despite 'only' 956 bombers taking part. It was less effective, mainly due to poor weather conditions which hampered the bombers' aim significantly. The full might of RAF Bomber Command was rounded up once more for a third massive raid on 25 June 1942 – this time the target was Bremen. The exact number of aircraft used in this raid is unverified, with some sources saying it was slightly more than a thousand machines, whereas others suggest it was slightly less. What we do know is a lot of aircraft flew over Bremen and dropped bombs that night. The raid was again blunted somewhat due to bad weather, but significant damage was still created; over 6,500 houses were either destroyed or damaged and eighty-five people were killed. At the Focke-Wulf factory, an assembly shop was completely flattened, and seventeen other buildings were damaged to varying degrees.

As a PR exercise in showcasing the power and might of the RAF and capturing the imagination of the British public, the raids were a success. But, apart from terrifying the population of the three cities, the raids achieved little in terms of strategic military value. Future RAF raids would concentrate on effectiveness and accuracy rather than sheer brute strength. After Bremen there would never be another Thousand Bomber Raid.

Raids

1 **Cologne, 30 May 1942**
1,047 bombers

2 **Essen, 1 June 1942**
956 bombers

3 **Bremen, 25 June 1942**
1,067 bombers

64 Sinking the *Tirpitz*

Named after Grand Admiral Alfred von Tirpitz, the *Tirpitz* was a Bismark-class battleship commissioned into the fleet of the German *Kriegsmarine* (navy) on 25 February 1941. The sister of the famous *Bismarck* battleship, the *Tirpitz* was similarly armed with a main battery of eight 38-centimetre (15-in) guns mounted on four turrets, along with a tranche of other guns ranging from 15 cm to 2 cm (Flak) guns, and eight torpedo tubes. After a series of wartime modifications, she was 2,000 (imperial) tonnes heavier than *Bismarck,* making her the heaviest battleship ever built by a European navy.

The reality was, however, that the *Tirpitz* didn't really see a lot of wartime action. The only time the crew of the *Tirpitz* fired her guns in anger was in September 1943 when, along with the battleship *Scharnhorst,* she bombarded Allied positions on Spitzbergen. One of the main reasons she was used so sparingly was the amount of fuel needed to keep her in service. In March 1942, the *Tirpitz*, along with the heavy cruiser the *Admiral Scheer* and several destroyers, attempted to intercept a couple of Allied Arctic convoys – using up 8,230 tons of fuel in the process. It took the Germans three months to replenish this fuel.

Therefore, the *Tirpitz* could often be found lurking quietly in one of Norway's deep fjords. However, she posed so much of a threat that the Allies were simply too scared to move any shipping between the North and Baltic Seas.

The Royal Navy had first attempted to sink the *Tirpitz* towards the end of September 1943 when they sent several X-class mini submarines to lay mines directly under the hull of the battleship. While the *Tirpitz* wasn't sunk, she was damaged, and it took six months for the repairs to be finished. After a few more failed attempts by the Royal Navy the baton was passed over to the Royal Air Force.

The first RAF attack took place on 15 September 1944 but was severely hampered by an effective smoke-screen that meant only one of the thirteen armour piercing 'tall boy' bombs that were dropped actually hit the target. A second raid took place on 29 October, but again was disrupted by low cloud. Despite the difficulties, damage was caused on both bomb runs and by the time the RAF made their third and final run at the *Tirpitz* she was nothing more than a floating gun battery unable to put to sea.

In the early hours of 29 November 1943, thirty-two modified Lancaster Bombers from the RAF and RAAF were heading straight for the *Tirpitz*. With about twenty miles left to run they spotted the battleship – there was no smoke screen, no low cloud and surprisingly, no protective fighter plane shield. At a distance of about thirteen miles, the massive guns of the *Tirpitz* opened up, quickly joined by coastal artillery and anti-aircraft guns. Approaching the target from anywhere between 12,000 and 16,000 feet the first 'tallboy' bomb was dropped at about 9.35 am local time. Within ten minutes the Lancaster crews had scored at least two direct hits and the *Tirpitz* was sinking.

Over the years the Allies had tried many, many times to sink the *Tirpitz* and failed; the Germans had believed her to be unsinkable. But by 10 am the *Tirpitz* had completely capsized with the loss of almost 1,000 men.

When the Secretary of State for Air, Sir Archibald Sinclair, visited the Squadrons at their base the day after the *Tirpitz* had been sunk, he congratulated them on sinking 'one of the toughest ships in the world'.

"When the force was about ten miles away the peaceful scene changed suddenly; the ship opened fire with her main armament and billows of orange-brown smoke, shot through by the flashes of the guns, hid her for a moment and then drifted away."

Wing Commander JB Tait DSO, DFC (617 Squadron, RAF)

Caught on camera

A special 463 Squadron RAAF Lancaster captained by Flight Lieutenant Bruce Buckham DFC RAAF was the last aircraft on the scene – the crew was tasked to film the operation. They went as low as 50ft and circled the crippled battleship several times, despite the shore batteries which remained in action after the *Tirpitz* herself had ceased firing.

D-Day from the air

Before anyone had set foot on the beaches on 6 June 1944, Bomber Command had already lost almost

300

aircraft and

2,000

attacking invasion targets.

During the Battle for Normandy the RAF flew

225,000

sorties at the cost of over

2,000

aircraft and

8,000

crewmen

1,800

RAF personnel and 456 RAF vehicles landed ashore on D-Day

5,656

Royal Air Force aircraft were involved in the D-Day landings.

In the first few weeks after D-Day Bomber Command averaged 5,000 sorties a week across Normandy.

By 9 June over

3,500

RAF personnel and 815 vehicles had landed in Normandy, working on airfield construction, aircraft servicing and forward controlling.

By the dawn of 6th June, Bomber Command had sent over a thousand heavy bombers to pound beach defences in Normandy with over 5,000 tons of bombs.

The unsung heroes of D-Day were

50

Squadrons of RAF Coastal Command kept the English Channel free of enemy submarines. Not one single Allied ship was sunk by the German Navy.

Fighters from Fighter Command protected the fleet and the beaches. Cover was so heavy that only two enemy aircraft managed to attack the beaches on the first day of the landings.

A small RAF Radar unit landed at Omaha Beach on D-Day to provide the radar and radio facilities to help direct R.A.F. fighter aircraft in defence of the beach-heads. This tiny unit won 4 Military Crosses and 2 Military Medals.

Jobs undertaken by the RAF on D-Day

Towing the Gliders of the British 6th Airborne Division in their assault on Bénouville Bridge

Dropping thousands of paratroopers deep into enemy territory to occupy other vital bridges and roads within the invasion area

Dropping thousands of dummy parachutists across Northern France to keep the enemy guessing as to the exact location of the invasion

Dropping tonnes of metal strips called 'window' across the English Channel to confuse and jam German radar

RAF Coastal Command patrolled the English Channel keeping it clear of enemy U-boats

Fighter Command flew constantly over landing zones to protect the invasion fleet and the beaches

Bomber Command bombers pulverised transport links and German reinforcements, destroying counter-attacks before they could start

Transport Command dropped supplies in from the air and took wounded soldiers back to safety

Radar units went ashore with the infantry to set up communication centres

65 D-Day from the air

As news of the Normandy beach landings started to filter back to Britain there was, not surprisingly, an insatiable appetite to follow what was going on in as much detail as possible. There were many news reporters working alongside the armed forces that day and their job was to record the moment with photos, written notes and audio reports.

There were also numerous other reports that came from men in the services that were directly involved in the invasion.

The first eye witness account to be broadcast from Normandy was from Air Commodore William Helmore, who at the time was flying above the D-Day beaches in a Mitchell bomber. The RAF were out in grand force strafing and bombing enemy lines, trying to cause as much disruption as possible.

Below is a written transcript of his report. The first eyewitness account broadcast from Normandy on 6 June 1944.

We're going across to bomb a target which is a railway bridge, which may help those good fellows down below in the boats. I know that it's what they do today that matters, but every little bit that the RAF can do to help is going to mean something.

We're coming down right low to attack our target; it's a pretty job, we're looking out for the markers now. I don't think I can talk to you while we're doing this job, I'm not a blinking hero. I don't think its much good trying to do these flash running commentaries when you're doing a dive-bombing attack. I can see flashes where the Bomber Command stuff is falling down: a lot of Bomber Command are pounding this invasion spot like hell, doing their best to tear it to pieces.

I've just heard the navigator say, 'OK. On it.' Now we're getting our nose down, and we've got to go down and give this bridge the works. We're in a colossal static storm at the moment, which is rattling in my ears like mad - what with the engine noise I can't hear myself speak at all. We're losing height rapidly - we're just going for it. There's something ahead of us there - do you see - do you see the light? Oh, I thought I was talking to the pilot, I recorded that. There's a funny light, I thought it was the markers going down - instead of talking into the intercom I talked into the record. I just heard the navigator say, over the intercom, 'We're over there', and I also heard the bomb-aimer say 'Shall I give it a cosh the moment I see it?' And the pilot said 'Yes'.

We're just going in to drop our bombs; it's a very tense moment — just the dawn of the moment when our troops are going in on the French beaches; I've seen them with my own eyes, practically in the act of touching down on the beaches. I feel it's a great privilege to be here. I'll be glad to get home all the same. Never mind, we're just getting ready to go in and bomb, and I'd better shut up. Hold It! My God, there's some bloody nasty flak round this place — very nasty flak, blast it!

Never mind, I heard the bomb-aimer say just now, 'Go in and do your stuff. Righto.' Ah, he hasn't let them off, I hear him telling the pilot to go 'straight and steady, straight and steady'. Oh, there they go — my God, what a good lift, what a good lift up into the air! We feel much lighter now. The best thing is to get out of here. We're pointed the right way round now anyway. Hell, the rear-gunner's reported — or the bloke at the back rather — has reported a night fighter after us. I hope we make this cloud ahead of us. I don't feel very belligerent. We're heading for the coast now. There's been a constant traffic of aircraft coming to and fro. Bomber Command's been out, we've passed a lot of them. There's great open patches in the cloud through which one can get a pretty good view. Now I can see the invasion craft out on the sea, like a great armada attacking France. This is history; it's a thing I can't be eloquent about in an aeroplane, because I've got engine-noises in my ears. But this really is a great moment for us, and to feel that I sit here with the weird means of telling you about what I'm seeing gives me a feeling of witnessing a strange pageant — something unreal. I feel detached, and that awful feeling that the great history of the world is unfolding before us at this very moment.

Air Commodore W. Helmore, RAF

Part of the invasion
coast at Normandy.

66 Operation Manna

In September 1944, the Dutch government, then exiled in London, called for a general rail strike in Holland in an effort to disrupt the movement of German troops around the country. The Germans retaliated by placing an embargo on food sent to occupied Holland. The larger cities relied for their food supply on soup kitchens, which gave out strict rations of food. However, when the months went on, the food became scarcer, especially potatoes and bread. The winter of 1944 was incredibly cold and by early 1945 the situation was becoming increasingly desperate for the three million Dutch people still under German control.

Originally the Allies were against the idea of any kind of food drop from the air because they feared that any supplies they delivered would just be taken by the Germans. But as more and more Dutch people started to die from starvation Prince Bernhard of the Netherlands appealed directly to Eisenhower, Churchill and Franklin D. Roosevelt in an effort to persuade the Allies to help. On 23 April 1945, authorisation was given to begin negotiations with German Reichskommissar, Arthur Seyss-Inquart, and it was eventually agreed that aircraft would not be fired upon as long as they kept to narrow, pre-designated air corridors.

On 29 April the first RAF Lancaster (nicknamed Bad Penny – as a bad penny always turns up) was loaded with food and supplies and took off in awful weather. On this day the ceasefire hadn't been formally agreed but despite this the crew flew incredibly low (down to 50 feet) over German gun batteries to deliver their cargo. Operation *Manna* had begun.

Between them RAF Lancaster and Mosquito bombers flew a total of 3,301 sorties between 29 April and 7 May 1945. Most of the supplies were dropped onto a few selected airfields, but as the supplies were not fitted with parachutes the crews had to deliver their cargo from incredibly low altitudes so as to limit damage. Most of what was delivered was tinned food, dried food and chocolate. Altogether, Bomber Command delivered 6,680 tonnes of food to the stricken Dutch.

In tandem with the RAF mission, the USAAF also flew over 2,000 sorties of their own, loading up B-17 Flying Fortress bombers with over 4,000 tonnes of supplies. However, despite the Allies together dropping over 11,000 tonnes of supplies, an estimated 20,000 people died of starvation.

"The idea was we would cross the Dutch border at 1,000 feet, and then drop down to 500 feet at 90 knots which was just above stalling speed... There was no truce at that point, and as we crossed the coast, we could see the anti-aircraft guns following us about. We were then meant to rise up to 1,000 feet, but because of the anti-aircraft guns we went down to rooftop level. By the time they sighted on us, we were out of sight. A lot of people were surprised we went without armaments, in case of any trigger-happy tail gunner."

RAF Navigator John Funnell

RAF Lancaster and Mosquito bombers flew

3,301

sorties and dropped

6,680

tonnes of food and supplies between 29th April and 7th May 1945.

A Lancaster drops food over Holland

National Liberation Museum Groesbeek

67 The Berlin Airlift

After WW2 the Allies split Germany into four zones – a Soviet Zone, a British Zone, an American Zone, and a French Zone. In June 1948, Britain, France and America decided to join their three Zones together into a new country – to be called West Germany – and on 21 June they introduced a new currency (the Deutsche Mark) for West Germany which they said would help improve trade. This move annoyed the Russians greatly as they feared it would undermine their policy of keeping Germany as weak as possible.

Three days later Stalin cut off all land and water routes through the Soviet Zone of Germany in and out of West Berlin, effectively isolating this area of the city. Despite claims that the Americans, French and British had a legal claim to use the highways, canals and rail networks that moved in and out of West Berlin across the Soviet Zone there was never a written agreement, so with West Berlin having just over a month's supply of food and forty-five days of coal, they were faced with a difficult decision: allow the inhabitants of West Berlin to starve or try and supply them through three 20-mile wide air corridors that had been formally agreed with Russia during the carve up of Germany.

It was calculated that almost 5,000 tonnes of supplies were needed per day in West Berlin to keep its 2,000,000 inhabitants alive. Due to post-war demobilisation the US Airforce had just ninety-three transport planes in the area that were capable of delivering about 300 tonnes a day. The RAF were in a slightly better position but could still only offer up to 400 tonnes a day – they were miles away from the 5,000-tonne daily target. Despite all of this an airlift was deemed the only viable way of relieving the situation and on 26 June 1948 USAF Dakota transport planes delivered 80 tonnes of food to the city. Two days late RAF Dakotas joined in. At that time, it was expected that the airlift would last three weeks.

During the first week, the airlift averaged 90 tonnes per day, during the second week the average went up to 1,000 tonnes. RAF Avro York transporters joined the airlift fleet, as did Sunderland flying boats from RAF Coastal Command. As the airlift continued the Allies improved their air traffic control systems as well as on-the-ground loading and unloading processes until the airlift system was a highly tuned process. At times aircraft were landing in Berlin every three minutes.

Although the Soviets did try to disrupt the airlift by many means such as shining searchlights at night to dazzle pilots, and aggressive flying or 'buzzing' by Soviet planes, there was nothing much the Russians could do to stop civilian planes landing and taking off from Berlin. Although the Soviet Army was much stronger than the Allies, the US had a stronger Navy and Air Force and they had nuclear weapons. No side really wanted another war.

In mid-April 1949, the Soviets hinted that they would be willing to lift the blockade. Negotiations were held almost immediately and a settlement was reached. The Soviet blockade of Berlin was lifted at one minute past midnight on 12 May 1949 although the airlift continued until September in order to create a stockpile of supplies.

In total over 2.3 million tonnes of supplies were airlifted into Berlin over a fifteen month period.

"Yaks (Soviet plane) used to come and buzz you and go over the top of you at about twenty feet which can be off putting. One day I was buzzed about three times.. The following day it started again and he came across twice and I got a bit fed up with it. So when he came for the third time, I turned the aircraft into him and it was a case of chicken, luckily he was the one who chickened out."

RAF planes flew almost

50,000

sorties to Berlin and covered over

18,000,000

miles

....

RAF planes delivered over

500,000

tonnes of food, fuel and equipment to Berlin

Former RAF Dakota pilot Dick Arscott

Royal Air Force Douglas C-47 Dakota transports being unloaded at Berlin Tegel airport

68 Operation Black Buck

The Avro Vulcan was going to be retired in 1982, but the outbreak of the Falklands conflict in the April of that year gave one of the most distinctive aircraft in RAF history a stay of execution. Not only that, but the old bomber was used in anger for the very first time to take part in not one but seven extreme long-range bombing sorties against Argentinian positions that have gone down in RAF folklore.

As the British Task Force sailed deep into the South Atlantic, discussions were afoot on how to effectively negate any Argentinian air threat. In particular, attention was focused on an airfield at Stanley on East Falkland. The runway was long enough for Argentinian fighters to use as well as transportation aircraft bringing in supplies to the occupying forces on the ground. One such option open to the RAF was to use the Vulcan for some kind of long-range bombing mission – so, just in case they were needed, three Vulcans were dispatched to RAF Ascension Islands.

However, it wasn't as simple as just sending the bomber on its way to smash the enemy. The base on the Ascension Islands was still thousands of miles beyond the maximum flight range of the Vulcan and it no longer had any mid-air refuelling capability. It required a round-the-clock engineering effort to hunt down the correct refuelling probes, re-manufacture the internal refuelling

systems and convert the bomb-bays back to pre-nuclear configuration to allow the carriage and delivery of conventional bombs. Once all this had been done it was agreed that the best way to deny the runway to enemy operations was to send one Vulcan, supported by several Victor tankers for air-to-air refuelling, which could hopefully carry out a successful bombing raid on the airstrip.

At 10.30 pm on 30 April 1982, the first of two Vulcan bombers fired up its engines and, followed by a back-up Vulcan, took off for Stanley airfield. Within minutes the lead Vulcan experienced technical difficulties and was forced to turn back. The entire operation now depended on Flight Lieutenant Martin Withers and his team in the second Vulcan, XM607. During their marathon journey south the Vulcan took on fuel five times but when an electrical storm hampered the last refuelling stop before the bomb drop the whole operation was close to being called off at the last minute.

In the Vulcan, Withers was furious as he consulted his crew as to what to do next. Shortly afterwards he made his decision, 'We're short on fuel, but we've come this far, I'm not turning back now.' At 290 miles away from the target, XM607 began a descent that would take them beneath the cover of Argentinian early warning radar systems. Then fifty miles from the airfield Withers pulled the Vulcan into a steep climb to 10,000 feet in an effort to avoid enemy fire – climbing like this would activate enemy radar, but Argentinian radar operators didn't call it in as they were convinced it was a friendly plane – the British fleet was still thousands of miles away. At 10,000 feet and travelling at 400 mph the target airfield was miniscule, two miles out they released the first of their bombs. When they had all been released Withers turned hard to the north and began the long haul back, hoping he could make it to the first refuelling rendezvous. They did make it and finally landed back at Ascension after a record-breaking sixteen-hour mission of nearly 8,000 miles.

The bomb run was successful with significant damage done to the airfield's installations and aircraft as well as to the runway itself. Three nights later a second raid took place (Black Buck 2) using the same aircraft but a different crew. On this raid the western edge of the runway was damaged preventing any extension of the runway. In all there were seven Black Buck missions – Black Buck 3 and 4 were eventually called off due to adverse weather and an issue with the refuelling unit respectively. Black Buck 5 took place on 31 May and targeted enemy radar installations. Black Buck 6 also attacked radar stations and finally on 12 June Stanley airfield was once again the target, just a few days before the battle for the Falkland Islands was over.

Date	Target	Successful
30 April / 1 May	Stanley Airfield	Yes
3 / 4 May	Stanley Airfield	Yes
13 May	Stanley Airfield	Called off
28 May	Radar Stations	Called off
31 May	Radar Stations	Yes
3 June	Radar Stations	Yes
12 June	Stanley Airfield	Yes

"This has never been done before; the eyes of the world are on you; there's a lot riding on this."

Final words from Air Vice Marshal George Chesworth to the crews of the first Operation *Black Buck*.

XM607

69 Operation Granby

In the early hours of 2 August 1990, Saddam Hussein ordered his Iraqi forces across the Kuwaiti border and on towards Kuwait City. Despite brave resistance, the small Kuwaiti Army were quickly overrun. Fearing that the Iraqis would march on into Saudi Arabia, American forces quickly began to appear in the region – this angered Hussein who then announced the formal annexation of Kuwait, declaring he was only willing to let it go if many demands were met.

The next few months saw an uneasy stand-off with the forces of thirty-three nations piling into the area to back up the Americans. A deadline was set for the Iraqis to withdraw their troops from Kuwait. If they were not out by 15 January 1991 the coalition forces would use 'all necessary means' to eject them. The deadline came and went with no movement from Saddam Hussein, at approximately 01:00 local time on 17 January, RAF Tornado GR1s with tanker support launched their first attack. Over the next six weeks the RAF, the USAAF and other coalition air forces subjected the Iraqi military to a sustained bombing attack that significantly reduced their fighting capability. As a result, when the ground troops commenced their advance on 24 February it took them just 100 hours to drive the Iraqi troops out of Iraq.

The RAF flew over

6,500

sorties during hostilities, dropping over

3,000

tonnes of weapons.

The Tanker Force offloaded some

13,000

tonnes of fuel, about three quarters of which was received by RAF aircraft, and one quarter by other Allied aircraft.

RAF Tornado GR1 aircraft were involved in the first wave of attacks on Iraqi airfields using the JP233 airfield denial weapon, 1,000 bombs and the ALARM anti-radiation missile. In the first 24 hours of offensive operations RAF aircraft flew a total of 101 sorties.

The Air Transport Force (ATF) flew around

13,000,000

miles in support of Operation Granby and moved some

50,000

tonnes of freight. Peaking at some

600 tonnes per day.

At the peak of hostilities some

5,500

personnel including reservists were deployed to the Gulf in support of RAF operations.

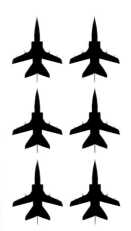

"The Gulf War was first and foremost an air power war and the RAF's contribution to the Allied air effort was significant and distinguished. The Service can take just pride in a remarkable feat of arms and a splendid professional achievement."

Group Captain Andrew Vallance - Director of Defence Studies for the Royal Air Force

A total of six Tornado GR1 aircraft were lost in combat during the conduct of air operations against Iraq.

RAF Gallantry Awards

Distinguished Service Orders

Distinguished Flying Cross

Mentions in Dispatches

Distinguished Flying Medal

Air Force Cross

70 Operation Herrick

Operation Herrick is the name given to all British military activity during the war with Afghanistan between 2002 and the end of combat operations in 2014.

In December 2001, the International Security Assistance Force (ISAF) was created to help the Afghan Transitional Authority in creating and maintaining a safe and secure environment in Kabul and its surrounding area. In 2003, NATO took over the running of ISAF and presided over a three-phase expansion of scope; the first two phases saw ISAF move into northern and western areas of Afghanistan and from 31 July 2006 it moved into the southern area of the country. It is here that the RAF provided major support to aid ISAF in its mission of facilitating reconstruction and the extension of government authority.

Approximately 850 RAF personnel were on the ground looking after a large number of different aircraft that all carried out different roles in the theatre. Tactical reconnaissance and close air support was provided by a force of Tornado GR4 aircraft; in-theatre airlift is provided by the RAF C-130 Hercules; air refuelling support for all coalition aircraft was provided by the Vickers VC10, while the Sentinel R1 and MQ-9 Reaper provided the RAF's Information, Surveillance, Target Acquisition and Reconnaissance (ISTAR) capability.

There was also a significant helicopter presence in Afghanistan with RAF Chinook and Merlin Helicopters providing vital land force transportation, ably backed up by the RAF Strategic Air Transport fleet moving men and material into and out of the region.

RAF Casualties during the war in Afghanistan

Flt Lieutenant Steven Johnson, 38
Flt Lieutenant Leigh Mitchelmore, 28
Flt Lieutenant Gareth Nicholas, 40
Flt Lieutenant Allan Squires, 39
Flt Lieutenant Steven Swarbrick, 28
Flight Sergeant Gary Andrews, 48
Flight Sergeant Stephen Beattie, 42
Flight Sergeant Gerard Bell, 48
Flight Sergeant Adrian Davies, 49
Sergeant Benjamin Knight, 25
Sergeant John Langton, 29

Sergeant Gary Quilliam, 42
Snr Aircraftman Christopher Bridge, 20
Snr Aircraftman Graham Livingstone, 23
Snr Aircraftman Gary Thompson, 51
Acting Corporal Marcin Wojtak, 24
Senior Aircraftman Kinikki Griffiths, 20
Senior Aircraftman Scott Hughes, 20
Squadron Leader Anthony Downing, 34
Corporal Brent John McCarthy, 25
Flight Lieutenant Rakesh Chauhan, 29,

Number of sorties flown on Op HERRICK by fixed-wing armed aircraft operated by the RAF (Source: Ministry of Defence)

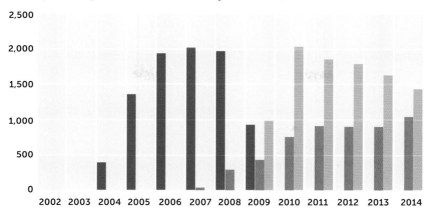

Number of flying hours and Weapon Release Events, and rate of Weapon Release Events, on Op HERRICK by fixed-wing armed aircraft operated by the RAF (Source: Ministry of Defence)

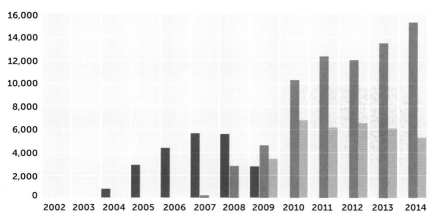

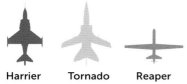

Harrier   Tornado   Reaper

Technological
Moments

71 The Sidcot Suit

Australian pilot, Sidney Cotton, flew night bombing sorties with the Royal Navy Air Service (RNAS) during WW1. On one particularly cold day at Ochey near Nancy, during the winter of 1916, he was ordered to scramble after spending time in the workshop working on his plane. That day he chose to fly in his oily overalls and upon his return, several hours later, he found that unlike all of the other pilots who were shivering from the cold, he was feeling pretty warm. He concluded that it must have been his overalls – or more to the point the oil and grease that had soaked into the overalls over the years – that had somehow enabled his body to retain more heat.

Cotton took advantage of this next block of leave from the front line to visit the Robinson & Cleaver department store in London where they made him a suit to his personal design. That particular suit consisted of three separate layers: a thin layer of fur, a layer of air-proof silk and a waterproof outside layer. The cuffs were lined with fur to stop warm air escaping from the suit and there were deep pockets designed into both knee and chest areas. The design of the suit was registered and was named directly after Sidney Cotton (Sidcot). Within four weeks of launch Robinson & Cleaver were making 1,000 suits a month and by 1917 the Sidcot Flying Suit had become a highly prized and indispensable piece of kit among RNAS and RFC pilots and

crew. They were also highly coveted by German aircrew and was the first item to be 'confiscated' from a British pilot taken prisoner. The German ace, Baron von Richthofen, was wearing one when he was shot down.

By 1920 the Sidcot Suit was fireproof and remained in use with the RAF during WW2 and only became redundant when fully enclosed cockpits and cabin heating became standard.

Keeps you warm at 20,000 feet up

The flying suit illustrated is designed to give perfect freedom to all movements. It is positively water and wind proof, light in weight and exceptionally warm. These points will be appreciated by practical aviators.

The "SIDCOT" Flying Suit

has seen Active Service and is the result of experience given to us by a well-known aviator.

Specification :—The cover is of specially prepared khaki twill interlined rubbered muslin lined mohair. With fur collar, as sketch **£9 9s.**

Give height, chest and waist measurement when ordering.

ROBINSON & CLEAVER Ltd.
REGENT STREET, LONDON, W.

The "SIDCOT".

First World War Sidcot Suits were proudly stocked and sold by London department store Robinson & Cleaver Ltd.

72 Pigeons

At the outbreak of WW2 thousands of pigeon fanciers across Britain gave up their birds for the sake of the war effort. In fact it is estimated that nearly a quarter of a million birds were used during the war, not only by the RAF but also by the army and the Civil Defence Service including the police, fire service and Home Guard. Pigeon racing was quickly suspended and along the coast of Britain birds of prey were culled so that any pigeon arriving back from France or beyond could arrive home safely.

All birds were enrolled into the National Pigeon Service, an organisation that reported into the RAF and was concerned with the distribution, protection and breeding of pigeons. The RAF considered pigeons a vital communication tool in times of emergency and pigeon lofts were built at all RAF bases – mobile lofts were also constructed so they could easily be transported to different areas.

The basic idea of the pigeon as a communication tool was simple. If the aircraft got into difficulties or was forced down in any way the crew would release the pigeon and it would fly back to its home base with details of the incident including location. All RAF bombers and reconnaissance aircraft carried at least one pigeon in special watertight baskets, and part of the pre-flight routine for the aircrew was to pick up their pigeon and a partially completed message template/form which gave details of the aircraft, home base and the date. In the event of an emergency the crew would quickly fill out the rest of the form with details such as their location, time, casualties etc. before releasing the bird. Pigeons carried their messages either in special containers on their legs or small pouches looped over their backs. Many airmen owed their lives to these heroic little birds.

The PDSA Dickin Medal was awarded to any animal displaying conspicuous gallantry and devotion to duty. During WW2 53 Dickin Medals were presented - 13 went to RAF Pigeons

73 The Parachute

On 1 March 1912, US Army Captain, Albert Berry, exited a Benoist pusher bi-plane high above a St Louis army base to become the first person to jump from an aeroplane and land by parachute. At that time, popular belief was that the only people crazy enough to use a parachute were showmen. Even in WW1 with the onset of aerial warfare the only men that were issued parachutes (or 'life savers' as they were known at the time) were the balloon observers who rode on tethered balloons to 'spot' for local artillery batteries. These balloons were something of a soft target for enemy aircraft so these 'life savers' were given out so the men could escape when attacked.

After the war the RAF showed little interest in the parachute for aircrew. They were of the opinion that if you gave a man a parachute he would be less inclined to try and save his plane in an emergency. Indeed research into it was cancelled in an effort to save money. In America, however, it was a different story and by 1921 all American aircrew were mandated to wear parachutes when flying.

By 1925, senior RAF figures were starting to warm to the idea of parachutes for aircrew and even sent a junior officer over to the USA to study their methods. Later that year an RAF parachute training course had been established and by

the end of May some sixty practice jumps had been made. Eventually an order was put in to America for 2,261 Irvin parachutes. Although the use of parachutes expanded during the late 1920s and 1930s it wasn't until WW2 that the use of a parachute was widely accepted, not just to save lives but also as a way to deploy ground troops deep into enemy territory.

74 Operation Varsity and The Caterpillar Club

Operation Varsity

The largest combat parachute drop was Operation *Varsity* – the Allied assault over the Rhine River - where over 16,000 British and American paratroopers dropped into various landing zones in and around the town of Wesel, Germany on 24 March 1945.

The Caterpillar Club

The Caterpillar Club is an informal association for people who have successfully bailed out of a disabled aircraft using a parachute. With people who qualify receiving a certificate and a caterpillar shaped lapel pin badge. The club was founded by Leslie Irvin of the Irvin Airchute Company (Canada) in 1922. At the end of WW2 the Caterpillar Club boasted over 34,000 members worldwide. Other parachute manufacturers set up their own Caterpillar Clubs too in subsequent years.

"Before you bailed out, you had to unbuckle, remove your radio plug and remove your oxygen feed. That took about ten seconds. Then, so that you didn't hit the tailpipe as you went, you had to roll the aircraft over on to its back, push the control column forward with your feet and eject yourself upside down."

Sergeant Leslie Batt. 238 Squadron, RAF

75 Variable Pitch Propeller

During WW1 there were huge strides made in aircraft development, design and technology. One such area that benefited from these improvements were the aircraft propellers (or airscrews as they were known at the time).

The role of the propeller was relatively simple; to convert the rotary power from the engine into propulsion and during WW1 almost all propellers were made from solid wood with a fixed pitch (or angle). During the war the Royal Aircraft factory at Farnborough figured out that if you could alter the pitch of the propellers during flight the engine would be more efficient, and the aircraft's performance would improve. Towards the end of the war the first variable pitch propellers were fitted onto a BE2C machine, however problems with the mechanical control to alter the pitch mid-flight meant those first propellers were not much good.

British engineers kept plugging away at producing a successful VP propeller and during the mid-1920s successful tests were carried out on a Gloster Grebe. Because there was not a great deal of interest from plane manufacturers the idea died a slow death.

Meanwhile, in America, the US Army Engineering Division were also developing a VP propeller system and by the early 1930s they had devised a system where the pitch could successfully and reliably be altered in-flight. The system was introduced in 1933 on the Douglas DC1 airliner, the first VP system to be produced commercially.

More development followed but unfortunately Britain was quickly left behind meaning that British aircraft manufacturers were forced to use the American version. But even so, the RAF was slow to recognise the advantages these new propellers could have on their aircraft. The first production models of both the Spitfire and Hurricane came with a two-blade fixed pitch propeller and it wasn't until 1939 that the fighters were fitted with a three-blade, two-speed metal propeller.

The new propeller gave the fighters an extra performance edge, especially the Spitfire which gained an extra 7,000 feet in altitude, an increase in climb rate and the ability to take off on a much-reduced take-off run. All of which came in very handy during the Battle of Britain.

ROTOL

In 1937, Rolls-Royce and Bristol Aeroplane Company formed the Rotol partnership to develop and build new variable pitch propellers to fit their latest range of engines – the Merlin and the Hercules.

76 Hispano 20mm Cannon

The Hispano 20mm Canon was perhaps the most important gun used by the RAF during WW2, although it had a rather less than auspicious start to its RAF career.

The Air Ministry had been discussing the need for the Hispano 20mm Canon in the absence of any British alternative. These discussions actually came from the idea that Air Staff were considering using armoured protection for RAF combat aircraft and the general consensus was that the Germans were probably having the same kind of conversations – in which case the old .303 rifle calibre rounds that were standard issue for RAF fighters just wouldn't be effective. They needed something with more firepower and an explosive 20mm cannon would make short work of any armour plating the Germans were cooking up.

The Hispano 20mm Canon was first used in the 1940 Westland Whirlwind, and the Bristol Beaufighter Nightfighter, and a small number were fitted to specially modified Spitfires during the Battle of Britain. However, in combat the gun was very prone to jamming, even after firing just one round, which made it virtually useless. The issues were pinpointed to the spring-driven magazine feed and this was changed in 1941 in favour of a much more effective belt feed mechanism which also increased ammunition supply to 750 rounds per minute.

As well as the Spitfire, aircraft such as the Hawker Hurricane, Typhoon and Tempest were all fitted with the Hispano Canon and by 1945 it had become the standard weapon for all RAF fighter planes.

Armourer loading Hispano cannon probably in the wing of a Spitfire

Hispano-Suiza No. Mk1 Cannon fitted to Hawker Hurricane

77 Helmore Turbinlite

The guiding principal behind the Helmore Turbinlite was a simple one. In order to help RAF fighters spot the enemy in bad weather or at night, why not have a plane flying with them that carried the latest radar equipment and had a large searchlight installed in its nose. Once this plane had locked onto an enemy machine, it could switch on its searchlight and bathe its target in such a strong glare that the pilot is blinded, and any accompanying RAF fighter can quickly shoot it out of the sky.

On paper it seemed like it would work, however, ultimately it would prove rather unsuccessful.

The brainchild of photo-reconnaissance pioneer Sidney Cotton and RAF Air Commodore Sidney Helmore they set about constructing the large flying searchlight. Because the carrying plane also needed to be equipped with the latest AI (Airborne Interception) radar which was also very heavy and bulky, there was no way this system could be installed into a fighter plane, so the apparatus was originally installed into a twin-engine Bristol Blenheim, but this plane was just too slow and unable to intercept any enemy aircraft.

Meanwhile, in the spring of 1941 the RAF started to receive a new plane from

A very big beam of light

The massive 1400amp light in the nose of converted Havocs could project a beam of light of 30 degrees divergence, 950 yards wide across a range of one mile. In order to not blind the pilot of the Havoc, hydraulically operated shutters were closed in and around the cockpit.

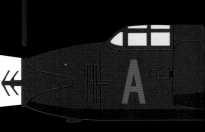

the USA – the Douglas Havoc twin-engine bomber – which offered a better alternative to the Blenheim, so it was decided to modify a few of these for testing.

The nose of the Havoc was modified to be able to take a 3ft-diameter disc of armoured glass. A 1,400-amp lamp with a para-elliptical reflector installed behind it that would project a beam over a mile in length. Such a powerful lamp generated a huge amount of heat and fumes, so a special ventilation system had to be designed and installed to stop the front of the Havoc melting. The batteries to power the light were stored in the Havoc's bomb bay – they had a combined weight of 1 ton and had enough juice to power the light for about two minutes. Approximately seventy planes were converted in this way and the Turbinlite went into active service in 1942.

Unfortunately, by January 1943 all Turbinlite converted planes were grounded having helped to shoot down only a single enemy aircraft. The concept behind the Turbinlite was rendered obsolete with the emergence of centimetric radar and high-performance night fighters such as the de Havilland Mosquito.

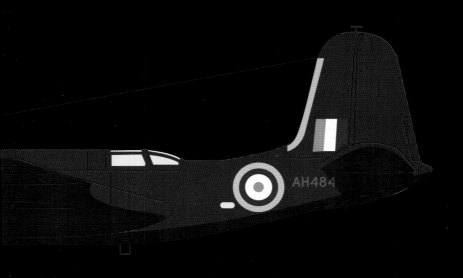

78 Gun Cameras

We have all seen those grainy black and white images and videos of dogfights between RAF fighters and German fighters or bombers – they are some of the most dramatic and authentic records of the Battle of Britain, perhaps even of the entire war. Those mesmerising images were captured by RAF Spitfires and Hurricanes that were equipped with the Williamson G42 wing mounted cine gun camera.

The gun cameras were not only used for propaganda purposes, they were also very useful in confirming pilot claims for kills. In the heat of a dog-fight, with aircraft flying about in all directions – some of whom were trying to kill you – it was sometimes difficult for a pilot to concentrate on and remember the details necessary to claim a kill in the debriefing room back at base. In the highly charged, competitive world of Fighter Squadrons there was considerable pressure on the young pilots to be seen to be contributing to the war effort, it was therefore very useful to have some kind of visual record to help confirm a kill claim. The G42 was not the perfect answer though as the camera was set to record only when the pilot pressed his fire button. As soon as he stopped firing the recording stopped.

Despite that the G42 was a considerable advancement on the aviation cameras of WW1 which were only able to take still shots and had to be manhandled by a crew member in flight. With the thicker wings of the new design of fighters entering service in the late 1930s, there was room for the camera to be inserted directly within the wing and aligned with the guns.

The G42 and the subsequent G45 were manufactured by the Williamson Company of London and Reading using 16mm orthochromatic film with a variable frame speed of either 16, 18 or 20 frames per second, depending on which machine gun the camera was linked up with. The camera itself was operated via an electrical switch, triggered by the gun-firing mechanism. The only thing the pilot of the plane had to do was to alter a switch in the cockpit to either 'sunny' or 'cloudy' in an effort to optimise the exposure.

The G45 continued to be used post war and in-wing cameras were only superseded with the advent of video recording being integrated into Head Up Display units.

> **"I remember one case where a man made a claim – even though he hadn't spent any ammunition."**

Flight Lieutenant Gerald Edge, 610 & 41 Squadrons, RAF

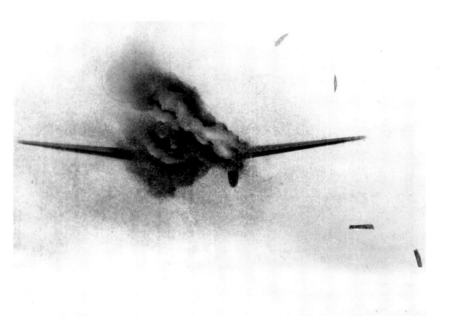

Still from gun camera film shot by Flight Lieutenant A G "Sailor" Malan, leader of 'A' Flight, No. 74 Squadron RAF, recording his first aerial victory, a Heinkel He 111 over Dunkirk. Although debris and billowing smoke issue from the Heinkel's starboard engine and the starboard undercarriage has dropped, Malan's claim was categorised as unconfirmed since he did not observe the aircraft's destruction

79 Upkeep – the Bouncing Bomb

For a number of years before the start of WW2 the Air Ministry had been gently exploring different ideas for destroying enemy dams and other large structures. Quite independently, Barnes Wallis, the then assistant chief designer at the Vickers-Armstongs Aviation section had also been looking at similar ideas including air-launched weapons. Initially, Wallis had worked on designing a huge bomb that would be dropped from a great height, creating a destructive shockwave underground but there was simply no plane available that could carry and deliver such a monster weapon, so he was forced to give up on that idea.

Instead he turned his attention to deploying a bomb against the surface of a dam which would cause a shockwave big enough to weaken it; his thought being that if enough of these weapons struck the dam it would then be destroyed. Trials began in 1942 to determine how much explosive would be needed and how to deliver such a weapon accurately. Early conclusions suggested it might be possible to drop a spherical bomb at low altitude in such a way that it actually bounced across the water to its target. In addition, if the bomb was spinning backwards it would help stabilise its journey across the water, allowing it to eventually sink close to the target. Wallis also concluded that about 6,000lb (2,720kg) of explosives, using a hydrostatic fuse like those found in depth charges (with a back up chemical time fuse) would be enough to do damage.

In November 1942, it was decided to commission larger versions of Wallis' design for attacks against dams, and smaller versions for attacks against ships – these were codenamed Upkeep and Highball respectively. Both were to be developed simultaneously, however, the Upkeep project had a definite deadline since the maximum effectiveness against the target dams in the Ruhr were dependent on them being as full as possible from seasonal rainfall – the latest day was pencilled in as 26 May 1943.

Testing of inert barrel-shaped Upkeep prototypes were carried out at Chesil Beach, Dorset in December 1942 and at Reculver in April and May 1943 – initially using a Vickers Wellington bomber – but it was soon discovered that only a modified Lancaster would be able to carry the bomb. The modifications included removal of the bomb doors to mount the spinning gear, the removal of the mid-upper gun turret to shed weight and the installation of the spinning gear and a hydraulic motor to power it. Wallis was also very insistent that the weapon be dropped 400–450 yards away from the target from a height of just 60ft (18m) with the aircraft maintaining a steady 220mph (350kmh). In addition to this, the bomb should be 'spun up' to 500rpm ten minutes before deployment to give it the backspin required. Such exacting requirements caused a lot of people high up in the Air Ministry to dismiss Wallis and his bouncing bomb invention as nothing more than fantasy.

Despite the naysayers, on 13 May 1943 a fully armed version of Upkeep was spun and dropped in a live trial just off the Kent coast. The bomb bounced seven times over some 800 yards, sank and detonated. Three days later nineteen modified Lancaster bombers from 617 Squadron took off loaded with Upkeep to attack dams in Germany's Ruhr Valley. Two dams were breached causing widespread flooding, damage and loss of life.

Upkeep was not used again operationally and by the time the war had ended the remaining Upkeep bombs had started to deteriorate and were dumped into the North Sea without their detonation devices.

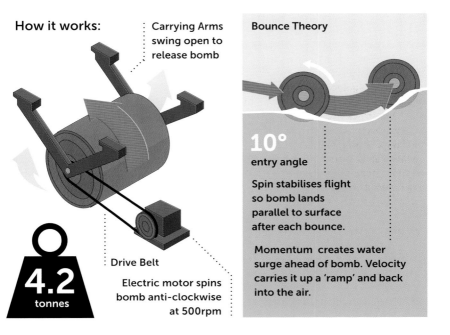

How it works:

Carrying Arms swing open to release bomb

4.2 tonnes

Drive Belt

Electric motor spins bomb anti-clockwise at 500rpm

Bounce Theory

10°
entry angle

Spin stabilises flight so bomb lands parallel to surface after each bounce.

Momentum creates water surge ahead of bomb. Velocity carries it up a 'ramp' and back into the air.

80 Chain Home and Chain Low Radar

In 1935 a radio scientist at the National Physical Laboratory by name of Robert Watson-Watt wrote a thesis entitled 'The Detection of Aircraft by Radio Methods' and, in an effort to prove his theory, he set up an experiment to try and detect a passing bomber using radio waves. On 26 February 1935, he successfully tracked a Handley Page Heyford bomber for eight miles using reflected radio waves that were received and displayed on a cathode ray oscilloscope, thereby proving his theory was possible.

The work Watson-Watt had carried out came to the attention of Sir Henry Tizard who headed up a committee concerned with air defence. Watson-Watt was made superintendent of a newly-formed establishment controlled by the Air Ministry – Bawdsey Research Station near Felixstowe in Suffolk. From here Watson-Watt started work on the design, the construction and installation of a chain of early warning systems around the coast of Britain that were to become known as Chain Home radar.

Essentially, radar works in much the same way that bats use sound waves (or echolocation) to 'see' in total darkness. The radar transmitter produces strong pulses of radio energy that are transmitted through the air by a directional antenna. When pulses hit an object, such as an aircraft, they are reflected back. These reflections are received by a radar antenna and converted by a receiver to an electric signal that can be displayed to the operator.

In the late 1930s, the technology to generate high-power pulsed radio energy at wavelengths short enough to make narrow beams did not exist. Instead, Chain Home relied on antennae that illuminated a huge area, just like a floodlight. These antennae did not move or scan at all. Rather, Chain Home radar operators chose a target ('blip') on their screen and turned the knob of a special instrument (called a radio goniometer) to minimise the blip. From this they could read the direction to their intended target from a scale around the knob. Although it required intense human interaction both to direction-find on each target and to filter the reports from many radar stations into a coherent air picture, the Chain Home system was highly effective. But the Chain Home system was only effective against aircraft flying at high altitude. In tests, RAF pilots had noticed they could escape detection by flying at low altitudes. This was due to the minimum angle of the CH being about 1.5 degrees above the horizon, which meant aircraft were below the radar's sight until they were within a few miles. At first this was not considered to be a serious limitation as bombers typically flew at altitudes of 15,000 feet or greater, and at that altitude they could be detected over France. However, the German's soon figured it out and started a series of low-level attacks that proved almost impossible to defend against.

To counter this threat, Watson-Watt took a similar system that was being developed for coastal defences and placed it next to his Chain Home stations. The new units (called Chain Home Low) filled the altitude gap and could also be turned to face inland, unlike the CH units which were constantly facing out to sea. Originally the antennae were moved manually, using wheel-less bicycles whose chains were connected to a gear system, but they were quickly motorised. There were also some mobile units which could be placed on trucks, extending the RAF's options in monitoring and engaging with the enemy.

By the outbreak of war in September 1939, there were twenty operational Chain Home stations. After the Battle of France in 1940 more were built, expanding the network of Chain Home and Chain Low stations from Orkney in the north to Weymouth in the south, providing effective radar coverage for the entire Europe-facing side of the British Isles.

The opening of the Russian Front had diverted much of Germany's bomber efforts and, except for one or two exceptions, the Luftwaffe never again attacked on the scale of the Battle of Britain or the Blitz. At the same time modern technology, the expansion of the radar system overseas and the requirement for skilled personnel for airborne radar had put the radar manpower situation under strain. In order to ease this strain and release the skilled personnel it was decided in November 1943 that the Chain Home system would be reorganised:

1. **Some stations would continue full operation,**

2. **Some stations would operate reduced watches and track handling,**

3. **Some stations would be placed on care and maintenance and,**

4. **Some stations would be dismantled.**

And so began the run-down of the world's first air defence radar system. Chain Home continued in operational use into the mid 1950's when it was finally replaced by new technology.

Chain Home and Chain Low Stations

Key

- Original 20 CH stations
- Added CH Stations
- Added CHL Stations

Sumburgh

Gaitnip
Netherbutton
Thrumster

Rosehearty
Hillhead
Doonie's Hill
School Hill

Douglas Wood
St Cyrus

Danstruther

Cockburnspath
Drone Hill
Bamburgh
Cresswell
Ottercops Moss

Glenarm

Shotton
Danby Beacon

Gregneish

Staxton Wold
Flamborough Head
Easington
Stenigot

Prestatyn
Ingoldmels

West Beckham
Happisburgh
Stoke Holy Cross
Hopton
Dunwich

Haycastle
Strumble Head

Walton
Canewdon

St Twynells
Warren

Whitstable
Foreness

Carnanton
Dunkirk

Worth Matravers

Rye
Dover

Dry Tree

Ventor
Poling

Pevensey

Rame Head

Hanks Tor
West Prawle

Truleigh
Fairlight

Bromley
Bawdsey
High Street

Beachy Head

81 Fog Investigation and Dispersal Operation (FIDO)

Fog shrouding airfields was a continual problem for the pilots of the RAF returning from bombing, reconnaissance and interception missions. It was particularly bad for the bomber crews who would return home, exhausted from a long and dangerous mission, where they had run the gauntlet of enemy fighters and anti-aircraft fire, only to find their base completely hidden by thick fog. Short on fuel and often limping home in damaged aircraft, many were forced to crash land. Not surprisingly this took a heavy toll on both men and machines.

The problem was so bad that in 1942 the Prime Minister got involved and challenged the Petroleum Warfare Department (PWD) to find a solution. Quickly.

The result was FIDO – Fog Investigation and Dispersal Operation – one of the most remarkable innovations of WW2. FIDO was a system of fuel tanks, pipes and rows of burners running the length of a runway. Once lit, it created huge lines of flames either side of the runway that were visible to pilots some sixty miles away, while the heat could disperse the thickest fog in a matter of minutes. After successful trials at the Pathfinder airfield at Graveley, Cambridgeshire, in April 1943 the FIDO system was installed across fourteen more airfields in England as well as at Epinoy in France.

All in all, it is estimated that this system enabled 3,000 Allied aircraft and some 15,000 crew members to make safe landings when their airfields were shrouded in fog. However, these safe landings came at a huge cost. The fires had to be kept burning otherwise the fog would roll back in, and as a result the system consumed vast quantities of fuel – a precious commodity in times of war that had to be transported in via tankers across the U-Boat riddled Atlantic Ocean – often at great cost to lives and shipping. After the war there were some conversations about installing a FIDO system at Heathrow, but it was scrapped due to the high operating costs.

> **On 16 November 1944, during a huge daylight bombing raid behind enemy lines, orders were given to fire up FIDO at RAF Woodbridge at 11.35 am after the weather deteriorated to aid the returning aircraft. Over the next seven hours some 85 fighters and bombers landed safely thanks to the FIDO system as it burnt away the fog. During this session it used over 700,000 gallons of fuel – enough to fill the tanks of more than 330 Lancasters.**

82 The Dowding System

During RAF exercises in 1937, closely monitored by the Commanding Officer of Fighter Command Hugh Dowding, it became very clear that pilots were not getting the information they needed to intercept enemy aircraft quickly and efficiently. This realisation led to Dowding setting up the Dowding System – the world's first modern command and control system.

The Dowding System brought together a network of radar stations, the men of the Royal Observer Corps, seven divisions of anti-aircraft artillery, balloon operations, command centres and one of the most intricate phone systems in existence, which allowed for the early detection of enemy airplanes and the communication of the details of their position and potential flight path to the right people. Quickly.

One of the keys to the success of the Dowding System was the way it filtered information, ensuring the pilots received information that was relevant to them. All information gathered from radar stations and members of the Royal Observer Corps, was submitted to the Fighter Command HQ (FCHQ) Filter Room located at Bentley Priory. Once the information was received and interpreted, it was then sent on to the relevant group.

During the Battle of Britain, Fighter Command was split into four main fighting Groups: 11 Group covering the south east of England and London; 12 Group covering East Anglia and the Midlands; and 13 and 14 Groups covering the north of England and Scotland. Each Group HQ would have their own plotting room with a detailed map of their area. When information about enemy aircraft was sent through from FCHQ it would be marked on large maps and plotting tables.

Each Group was further split into Sectors. Once Group HQ had received information from FCHQ they would inform the relevant Sector Stations, which would house the Sector Command Post. Once a Sector had received word from Group HQ they would scramble their fighters and get airborne as quickly as possible. Once in the air the pilots would be given detailed information about the range, heading, altitude and number of enemy aircraft to expect. The end result was a huge increase in overall RAF effectiveness. Before the war, interception rates of fifty per cent were considered excellent form, during the Battle of Britain the average rate of interception by Fighter Command was eighty per cent.

The Dowding System turned Fighter Command into a lean, mean intercepting machine and contributed greatly to the success of the RAF against the *Luftwaffe*.

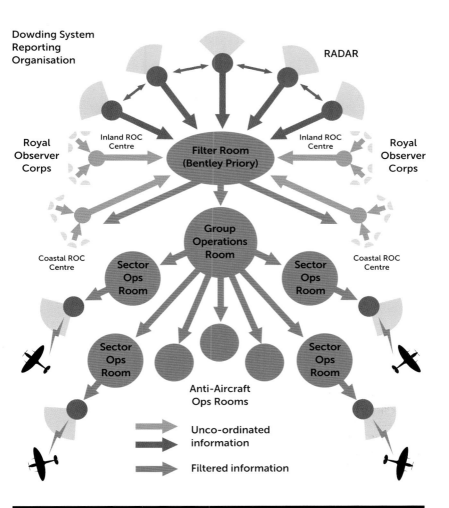

Dowding System Reporting Organisation

RADAR

Royal Observer Corps

Inland ROC Centre

Filter Room (Bentley Priory)

Inland ROC Centre

Royal Observer Corps

Coastal ROC Centre

Group Operations Room

Coastal ROC Centre

Sector Ops Room

Sector Ops Room

Sector Ops Room

Sector Ops Room

Anti-Aircraft Ops Rooms

Unco-ordinated information

Filtered information

"All the ascendancy of the Hurricanes and Spitfires would have been fruitless but for this system which had been devised and built before the war. It had been shaped and refined in constant action, and all was now fused together into a most elaborate instrument of war, the like of which existed nowhere in the world."

Sir Winston Churchill

83 Chaff Countermeasures

Originally called 'Window' by the British when first developed in WW2, Chaff is a radar countermeasure in which aircraft or other targets dispense a cloud of small strips of aluminium or metallised paper or plastic into the air which confuses enemy radar stations with hundreds of false readings.

It may seem unlikely, but this relatively simple procedure was one of the single most important radio countermeasures of WW2. Germany and Britain were developing similar ideas at the same time, however they were all reluctant to use Window (or Düppel as the Germans called it) in case the enemy discovered it, copied it and launched their own huge bombing raids. The British authorities were especially worried of another Blitz, however, when Fighter Command received new centimetric radar systems in the summer of 1943 it was felt they could cope with a German retaliation. Arthur 'Bomber' Harris (Commander-in-Chief of Bomber Command) eventually got permission from the government to use Window as part of the planned 'fire raids' on Hamburg.

The first aircrew to be taught how to use Window were part of 76 Squadron. Twenty-four crews were selected and shown how to drop bundles of aluminised paper strips at one-minute intervals through the flare chute. The first raid to use Window took place over Hamburg on 24/25 July 1943. The results were spectacular, totally paralysing and confusing the German defensive system, allowing the bombers to wreak havoc on their targets with minimal enemy interference. German radar-guided searchlights wandered aimlessly across the skies, anti-aircraft guns fired randomly or not at all and the night fighters, who relied on their radar to track down enemy bombers, were swamped with false readings and failed to find the actual bomber formations. Out of 791 bombers sent over to Hamburg, only twelve were lost.

Over the coming weeks the German home defences were able to get themselves better organised but even so Window remained a constant thorn in the side of the Luftwaffe. Initially bundles of Window were just shoved down the flare chute by the wireless operator, but later in the war automatic dispensers were built into the undercarriage of aircraft to make the release more accurate.

Window (or Chaff as it is now known as) is still used today to distract radar-guided missiles from their targets. Most military aircraft and warships have chaff dispensing systems and many intercontinental ballistic missiles will release decoy balloons and chaff mid-course in an effort to confuse enemy counter-measures.

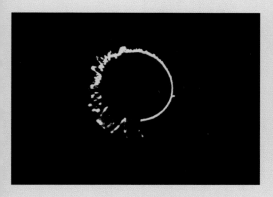

The effect of chaff on the display of a Würzburg Riese radar. The effect of jamming appears in the left "jagged" half of the circular ring, contrasting with the normal "smooth" (unjammed) display on the right half of the circle, with a real target at the 3 o'clock position — on the jammed left side the real target "blip" would have been indistinguishable from the jamming

A Lancaster bomber dropping 'Window', the tin foil strips that appeared as a mass of aircraft on German radar

84 Rolls Royce Merlin Engine

Arguably one the most important aero engines ever built, the Rolls Royce Merlin Engine started life as a private venture project within Rolls Royce after they failed to get government funding to help with its initial development as they worked to build a bigger, more powerful engine than the 21-litre Kestrel engine that was in service in the early 1930s.

Codenamed PV-12 (Private Venture, 12 cylinders) the engine was first tested in anger in 1935 and after numerous developments the first production engines (Merlin I) took to the air on 10 March 1936 bolted to a Fairey Battle – a single-engine light bomber.

The Merlin I was tweaked further to become the Merlin II – the first of the main production engines developing 1030hp at 5,500ft. The Merlin II found a home inside large numbers of RAF planes including two new fighters, the Hurricane and the Spitfire. The engine continued to be developed rapidly in order to keep up with the demands of the war and was used in over forty planes, including the Avro Lancaster, Vickers Wellington, Handley Page Halifax, de Havilland Mosquito, Bristol Beaufighter and a variation of the P-51 Mustang.

Because of such insatiable demand, production was spread all across the UK and even produced under licence in the USA by Packard. By the end of the war around 150,000 engines had been built.

Some of the aircraft using the Merlin Engine:

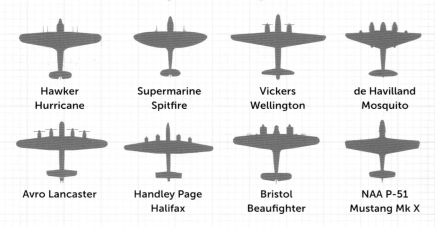

| Hawker Hurricane | Supermarine Spitfire | Vickers Wellington | de Havilland Mosquito |

| Avro Lancaster | Handley Page Halifax | Bristol Beaufighter | NAA P-51 Mustang Mk X |

Merlin Engine

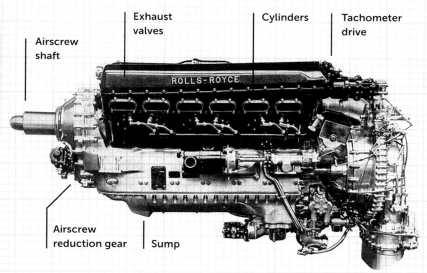

Airscrew shaft

Exhaust valves

Cylinders

Tachometer drive

ROLLS-ROYCE

Airscrew reduction gear

Sump

Engine type: Liquid Cooled V12 piston aero engine with supercharger

Manufacturer: Rolls Royce

Capacity: 27 litres / 1,650 cu inches

Cylinders: V12

Power: 1,000hp – 2,030hp

Numbers built:

149,659

First production flight:

10 March 1936
(Fairey Battle)

"When you jump into the aeroplane and start up the Merlin engine, there's a bang and a roar and you're hyped up and you know no one's going to shoot you down. That's for sure."

Pilot Officer Archibald Winskill, 72 and 603 Squadron, RAF

85 The Jet Engine

In 1926 a young RAF apprentice by the name of Frank Whittle was recommended for officer training. Part of his course required him to write a thesis and his was entitled 'Future Developments in Aircraft Design'. In this paper, Whittle argued that a new engine design was needed if the increased demand for aircraft that could fly higher and faster than currently possible was to be met. In that paper he laid down the fundamental ideas of a new way of powering flight – the jet engine.

Despite winning prizes for his academic prowess, the RAF ultimately rejected his idea and after failing to convince the engineering firm British Thomson-Houston (BTH) to take up the idea he went back to concentrating on his flying career.

Meanwhile, conversations regarding the potential of Whittle's design still took place and in 1936 with the help of the Air Ministry he formed the company Power Jets Ltd. First tests were carried out a year later and in 1939 the Air Ministry gave the official green light that allowed Whittle to concentrate on developing his engine full time. However, all of these delays had resulted in Germany catching up and even surpassing British development levels.

Known as the W1, the Whittle engine featured a central compressor surrounded by ten small combustion chambers. It was ready for testing a couple of years later and on 15 May 1941 a small aircraft built by Gloster (codenamed E28/39) with the jet intake housed in its nose, made the first test flight of the W1 turbojet engine.

The lessons learned from the E28/39 test flights paved the way for Britain's first operational jet fighter – the Gloster Meteor – which entered service in the summer of 1944 and was the Allies' only operational jet aircraft of WW2.

The first British jet powered flight

Date – 15 May 1941

Aircraft – Gloster E28/39

Pilot – Gloster's Chief Test Pilot, Flight Lt Gerry Sayer

Duration:	Max Speed:
17	**350**
minutes	**mph (563kmh)**

Whittle W1 Engine

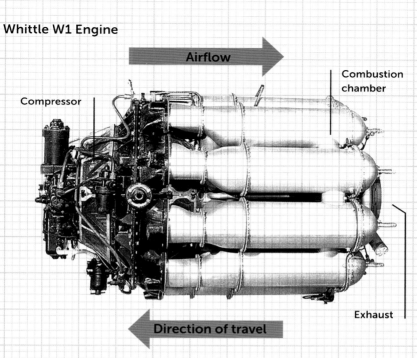

Airflow

Compressor

Combustion chamber

Direction of travel

Exhaust

Gloster E28/39

The first British jet engine to fly developed 1,032lb of thrust

Britain's first jet squadron

On 12 July 1944, 616 Squadron, based at RAF Culmhead, swapped its Spitfires for Gloster Meteors to become Britain's first jet squadron.

86 Ejection Seat

The modern ejection seat can trace its ancestry right back to WW2. Until then the only way to exit an aircraft during flight was to jump(!), however in situations where there were high G-forces or severe wounds, this was often impossible. This situation led the brightest minds on both Allied and Axis sides to work towards a system that propelled a pilot or crew member clear of their aircraft in emergency situations.

The first recorded ejection from an aircraft took place in Germany in 1942, meanwhile in Britain, James Martin and Valentine Baker, owners of the Martin-Baker Aircraft Company, started to investigate for themselves the options available around ejection seats. When Valentine Baker was killed on a test flight on 12 September 1942, Martin's primary focus became aircrew safety and under his stewardship the company was completely reorganised to focus solely on the design and manufacture of aircraft ejection seats.

In 1944 Martin was invited by the Ministry of Aircraft Production (MAP) to investigate equipping RAF fighter aircraft with a means of assisted escape for the pilot. Development of the seat was rapid with Martin concentrating on the principle of using an explosive charge to force the seat up and out of the aircraft with the occupant still in it. Once safely clear of the aircraft the pilot could then open

his parachute. On 24 January 1945, the first test ejection was carried out from a static test rig and eighteen months later, on 24 July 1946, they successfully carried out their first mid-flight test ejection using a Gloster Meteor flying at 320mph (510km/h) at 8,000ft (2,400m).

In June 1947, the MAP declared that all new RAF aircraft were to be fitted with the Martin-Baker Mk1 Ejection Seat as standard. Those early seats had an adjustable seat pad that could be raised and lowered to suit the height of the occupant without moving the seat itself. It also had foot rests and thigh guards to stop leg injury on ejection, which was caused by the pilot pulling on a red handle. Once pulled the seat was guided by rollers up and out of the cockpit at a rate of 60ft/sec. Once the seat had risen 24ft a small parachute attached to the seat opened which slowed the ejection down enough for the pilot to unclip himself from his seat and activate his own personal parachute.

Seat development was constant and on 15 July 1952 the first ejection was made with the MkII fully automatic seat. In the early years, a successful ejection was dependent on the plane moving forwards but over the years further development meant that a safe ejection was possible in virtually any situation, including being completely stationary on the ground with the 'zero-zero' seat which was introduced in the early 1960s.

How an ejection seat works

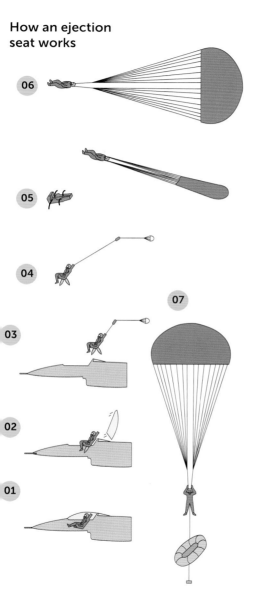

The Martin-Baker MkI seat saved the lives of

69

aircrew

In 1987 Martin-Baker introduced the first micro-processer controlled ejector seat

Over **7,500** lives have been saved as a direct result of Martin-Baker ejection seats

The Ejection Tie Club

Martin-Baker ran an exclusive club for those airmen who had safely ejected from an aircraft using a Martin-Baker ejection seat. Every club member was given a certificate, membership card, patch, tie, and a pin badge. All Tie Club memorabilia depicts a red triangle, the international danger symbol for an ejection seat. Currently there are over 6,000 registered members.

87 Identification Friend or Foe (IFF) system

On 6 September 1939, Spitfires of 74 Squadron along with Hurricanes of 151 Squadron were scrambled to intercept unidentified enemy raiders. In the engagement some of the Spitfires opened fire on a couple of Hurricanes, one of which was piloted by twenty-six-year-old Pilot Officer Montagu Hutton-Harrap. Harrap's machine crashed near Ipswich claiming the life of the young officer. This tragic incident highlighted the shortcomings of many aspects of Fighter Command at that time including its control system, Observer Corps reporting, radar and indeed fighter intelligence when under pressure. However, it did ultimately lead to the introduction of the IFF Identification System.

Even though the RAF had a good radar system, it was not able to distinguish between enemy aircraft and home squadrons; something else was needed so the man behind the idea of radar (Robert Watson-Watt) began working on some kind of identification system.

The first version of the system – the IFF Mk1 – was ready just in time for the Battle of Britain, but in reality, only a handful of RAF fighters had the system installed. The concept is simple. An IFF interrogator (a kind of secondary radar) sent a request signal by radio to the aircraft in question. A special piece of equipment on the aircraft called an IFF 'transponder' picked up the signal and gave a response to identify itself as 'friendly'. If nothing came back, the

How it works

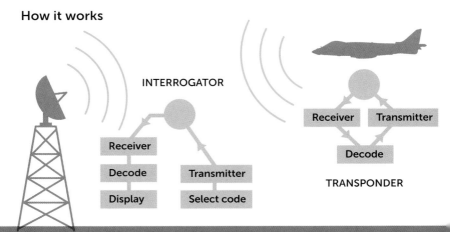

INTERROGATOR

Receiver

Decode

Display

Transmitter

Select code

Receiver   Transmitter

Decode

TRANSPONDER

plane was probably hostile. Those early systems used a single set frequency that had to be manually reset as they moved between stations – this was awkward for the pilot to do, especially if engaged with the enemy. Early IFF systems were quite unreliable.

Subsequent improvements to the IFF system resulted in a MkIII version, developed by the Telecommunications Research Establishment (TER) and introduced in 1941. It was a much more reliable and automated system and became the standard IFF system used by the Western Allies throughout the rest of the war.

The IFF system of the 21st Century is a two-channel setup used worldwide. One channel (1.03GHz) is used for the interrogating system, another (1.09GHz) is used for the reply. It is divided into five modes: Mode 1 is not fully secure and is used by ships to track aircraft and other ships; Mode 2 is used by aircraft landing on aircraft carriers in poor weather; Mode 3 is the standard civilian air traffic control system and Modes 4 and 5 are fully secure systems using sophisticated encryption techniques specifically for military aircraft.

In the modern age of supersonic aircraft and missiles, such a system is particularly important as it is impossible to rely solely on visual identification when targets are travelling at such speed.

"Quite early in the war, British aircraft were equipped with equipment known as 'IFF', 'Identification – Friend or Foe'. This meant that when our RDF pulses struck British aircraft, there was an immediate response from the aircraft transmitter which was picked up by the RDF station on its cathode ray tube. This operated every few seconds, indicating that the response was coming from a friendly aircraft. Any other aircraft being plotted were assumed to be enemy."

Aircraftman Wilfred Slack, Engineer

88 Grandslam Bomb

Invented by Barnes Wallis, the Grand Slam was a 22,000lb (10,000kg) 'earthquake' bomb used by RAF Bomber Command against strategic enemy targets during WW2. When released, the Grand Slam would reach speeds of over 700mph before burrowing deep underground. When it detonated, the resulting explosion would damage the target's foundations from underneath – hence it was dubbed the 'earthquake' bomb.

Its design was based on the slightly smaller 'Tallboy' bomb; each one containing over 4,000kg of explosives. The explosive was poured in when hot – it took a month to cool down and set – which meant production was slow and expensive. Not surprisingly, aircrews were told to land with their unused bombs on board rather than jettison them into the sea if a sortie was aborted.

The Grand Slam was first used on 14 March 1945 when Lancaster bombers from No. 617 Squadron RAF attacked the Bielefeld railway viaduct destroying large sections. By the end of the war forty-one Grand Slam bombs had been dropped, mainly against large structures such as bridges, bunkers and viaducts.

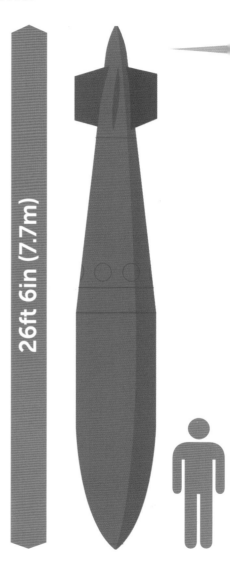

26ft 6in (7.7m)

Weight:
22,000lb
(9,979kg)

Warhead:
4,144kg
(9,135lb) Torpex explosive

Biggest Bomb of the War

With a blast equivalent to 6.5 tonnes of TNT the Grand Slam was the most powerful non-atomic aerial bomb used during WW2.

Numbers used:
41

"This 22,000lb bomb did not reach us before the spring of 1945, when we used it with great effect against viaducts or railways leading to the Ruhr and also against several U-boat shelters."

Sir Arthur 'Bomber' Harris

89 Blue Danube

After the end of WW2 the overall international situation was unstable to say the least. In the face of potential national threats from Russia and the real possibility of American isolationism, the British government were forced to kick start development of a viable nuclear deterrent.

Over a period of seven years a group of British scientists worked in utmost secrecy to produce a viable atomic weapon. Initially their work was based on the American 'Fat Man' bomb that was dropped on the Japanese city of Nagasaki in 1945, and in October 1952 the first British fission device was tested off Western Australia.

After more design tweaks to make the device operational as a bomb (including a protective casing and four fins on the tail to ensure a stable flight trajectory once released from a plane) and further testing at Maralinga, South Australia, the first of these weapons – codenamed 'Blue Danube' – was delivered to the Bomber Command Armament School at RAF Wittering on 7 November 1953. However, the RAF would have to wait another eighteen months before they had a working bomber that was capable of carrying and deploying this weapon.

On 15 June 1955, No. 1321 Flight, RAF took delivery of their very first Vickers Valiant B1 bomber to enable them to carry out performance testing of the new weapon and on 11 October 1956 the first British-built nuclear weapon was dropped from an aircraft from 30,000ft over the Maralinga test range in South Australia.

Despite serious design defects Blue Danube became Britain's first operational nuclear weapon with fifty-eight bombs produced (although not all of them were operational at the same time) before production ceased in 1958.

Blue Danube was retired from service in 1962 in favour of smaller, more reliable weapons such as Red Beard.

Britain's first Nuclear Bomb

The first live British nuclear weapon to be dropped from an aircraft took place at the Maralinga test range in South Australia on 11 October 1956. The bomb was carried by a Vickers Valiant B1 bomber and dropped from a height of 30,000ft.

24ft (7.3m)

Weight:
10,000lb
(5 tons)

Numbers built:
58

Explosive
equivalent :
14,000
tons of TNT

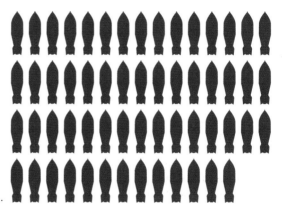

A Blue Danube bomb at the UK's first
atomic bomb store at RAF Barnham

Keith Eldred/PA

90 Yellow Sun

Hot on the heels of Blue Danube, the RAF's first nuclear weapon, came a series of nuclear weapon tests conducted at Christmas Island and Malden Island between 1956 and 1958 under the codename Operation *Grapple*. Out of the testing came a new weapon – called Yellow Sun – and it was to become Britain's first H-bomb.

First up was Yellow Sun Mk1 – an 'emergency' weapon that was never intended as a long term solution. Its warhead was the non-thermonuclear Green Grass which possessed a yield of 400 kilotons. However, the RAF deemed it unsafe and it was never tested.

It was always the plan to develop Yellow Sun further to include the Granite type warheads that had been tested during Operation Grapple, but in 1958 it was decided to abandon that plan and adopt the US W-28 warhead instead. Altered slightly to conform to British engineering practices, the warhead was eventually known as Red Snow.

Red Snow was smaller, lighter but more powerful than Green Grass and entered service as Yellow Sun Mk2 in 1961. Designed to be carried by the RAF's V-bombers, around 150 Yellow Sun Mk2 bombs were produced and they remained as the RAF's primary air-drop strategic nuclear weapon until the late 1960s.

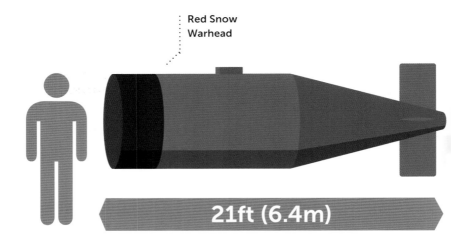

Red Snow
Warhead

21ft (6.4m)

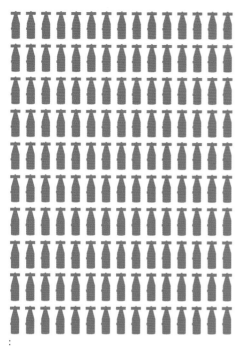

No Parachute

Unlike other contemporary bombs of similar power, Yellow Sun was not designed with a parachute to slow its fall. Instead, it had a blunt nose that induced enough drag to slow the weapon down enough for any bomber to get away in good time.

Warhead:

1.1 mt

(4.6 PJ)
Plutonium/
Hydrogen
Red Snow

Numbers built:

150

A Yellow Sun nuclear bomb at the Royal Air Force Museum, Cosford

Weight:
7,250lb
(3,290kg)

Tom Oates, 2011/WikiCommons

91 AAR – Air to Air Refuelling

Air-to-air refuelling is now commonplace in modern military aviation but it wasn't always that way. After WW1 aviation enthusiasts competed with each other in setting aerial long distance records, many using crude in-flight refuelling techniques which were nothing more than a piece of hose running from a hand-held fuel tank on one aircraft directly into the fuel tank of another. One such enthusiast was former RFC pilot and aviation pioneer, Alan Cobham, who began experimenting in the late 1920s with different ways of refuelling in an effort to extend his flight range.

In 1934, Cobham founded Flight Refuelling Ltd and went on to develop a range of equipment and techniques to aid in flight refuelling including the 'looped hose' method where a tanker aircraft lowered a weighted line down to an operator in the receiving aircraft flying below, this line was then used to pull the fuel hose down to the receiving craft. Once in position fuel would flow using gravity. Cobham originally saw his system as a way of aiding long distance civilian air travel and in 1939 fifteen Atlantic crossings were made utilising his refuelling system. Further trials had to be suspended due to the outbreak of war.

At the end of 1948, the USAF asked Cobham to work with them on a refuelling system that would work for single-seat fighter planes. Within months

he had developed a prototype of his 'probe and drogue' system, which saw the receiver pilot fly his probe nozzle directly into a conical drogue basket at the end of a fuel hose trailing from the tanker plane. As the nozzle entered the basket it opened a cut-off valve and allowed fuel to flow. The RAF also took interest in this new system and using a modified Lancaster bomber as a fuel tanker undertook trials with a Gloster Meteor F.3 jet fighter. On 7 August 1949 the Meteor set a jet engine endurance record by remaining airborne for twelve hours and three minutes flying 3,600 miles (5,800km) thanks to ten refuellings from the Lancaster.

In 1958, 214 Squadron based at Marham became the RAF's first air-to-air refuelling unit with a fleet of Vickers Valient B(PR) K.1 tankers – specifically designed to supply the Vulcan and Victor bombers. In 1966 it took delivery of new Handley Page Victor tankers and continued supplying in air fuel services until it was disbanded in 1977. The Victor carried on and provided a vital refuelling service during the Falklands War – eventually being retired from service in 1993 when they were replaced by Lockheed L-1011 and Vickers VC10 transports that were specially refitted to serve as tankers.

Currently the RAF utilise the Airbus A330 MRTT Voyager under the Future Strategic Tanker Aircraft Project.

The Voyager project will cost the MoD a cool £390 million over the course of the contract (until 2035). Totalling £10.5billion.

Two Royal Air Force Typhoon fighters from 29 Squadron (foreground), refuel from a VC 10 aircraft while a Tornado jet fighter waits in the background over RAF Akrotiri, Cyprus

On a typical deployment across the Atlantic, a single A330 would be able to refuel 4 RAF Tornados and still carry 11,000lb (5000kg) of freight/passengers.

6,000
miles

11,000
miles

In 1961 RAF Valiant tankers refuelled an Avro Vulcan bomber all the way to Australia.

92 AIM-9L Sidewinder Missile

Developed by the US Military way back in the 1950s, the AIM-9 Sidewinder is perhaps the most important missile of recent history, and the main air-to-air, short-range heat-seeking missile used by the RAF from the mid 1970s.

Although a complicated piece of weaponry the AIM 9L (Air Intercept Missile) is basically split into four sections. At the nose is the infrared guidance system, behind that is a target detector, then the high explosive warhead and finally the solid fuel rocket motor that can propel the missile to a speed of more than Mach 2.

Relatively cheap and simple to manufacture and maintain, the AIM-9 went through a series of performance upgrades in the early 1960s and by the time war broke out in Vietnam the missile had asserted itself as the standard short range air-to-air missile in the USAAF fleet. Although in reality it had little or no serious competition and in those early days of the Vietnam conflict reliability issues were commonplace. The missile was also really best suited to pursue slow moving bombers, not MiG fighters, although the Sidewinder accounted for destroying many enemy MiGs in Vietnam. It was the missile's performance in

> "I raised the safety catch and mashed the red, recessed firing button with all the strength I could muster... There was a fractional delay as the missile's thermal battery ignited (then) the Sidewinder was transformed from an inert, eleven-feet-long drainpipe into a living, fire-breathing monster as it accelerated to nearly three times the speed of sound and streaked towards the enemy aircraft."

**Flight Lieutenant David Morgan,
Sea Harrier Pilot, RAF.**

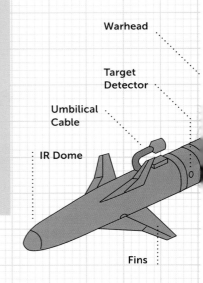

Warhead

Target
Detector

Umbilical
Cable

IR Dome

Fins

Vietnam that led the RAF to buy the AIM-9G during the 1970s for its own fighter planes. The AIM-9L was introduced soon afterwards and changed the face of air-to-air combat for good. Previously all heat-seeking missiles would need to be fired from behind the target to enable the missile to lock onto the heat from the plane's exhausts. With the AIM-9L that didn't matter; a target could be fired upon from any angle. The RAF quickly swapped out their AIM-9Gs for AIM-9Ls and by the mid 1980s all combat aircraft including the Harrier, Jaguar, Bucanneer and Tornado were equipped with AIM-9Ls.

During the Falklands conflict AIM-9L Sidewinders took care of eighteen Argentinian aircraft.

Phased out due to the introduction of the ASRAAM missile into the RAF's weapon inventory in 1998, the Sidewinder saw service for almost thirty years in Britain. Well over 100,000 missiles were built and many countries still use them today, some sixty years after they were first introduced.

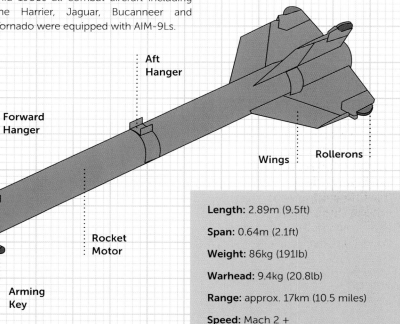

Aft Hanger

Forward Hanger

Wings

Rollerons

Rocket Motor

Arming Key

Length: 2.89m (9.5ft)

Span: 0.64m (2.1ft)

Weight: 86kg (191lb)

Warhead: 9.4kg (20.8lb)

Range: approx. 17km (10.5 miles)

Speed: Mach 2 +

93 Head Up Display

The Head Up display (HUD) allows a pilot to view vital instrument and weapon data without having to look down to the cockpit and instrument panel. Hence the term 'Head Up'. The Head Up display is widely regarded as one of the greatest innovations in cockpit design in the history of the fighter plane. Typical information that is shown on HUDs include airspeed, altitude, heading, horizon details and weapon data.

The overall concept originates from the reflector and gyro gunsight mechanisms from around the time of WW2. During the later stages of the war the Telecommunications Research Establishment (TRE), in charge of UK radar development, found that RAF night fighter pilots were struggling when looking up from a brightly lit radar screen into the dark sky and finding their target. By October 1942, they had successfully combined the radar image with a projection of the gyro gunsight onto a flat area of the windscreen; they were even able to add in an artificial horizon to help the pilot even more.

The Royal Aircraft Establishment, Farnham, developed the HUD concept further in the 1950s and soon Britain was leading the way in HUD instrumentation. By 1958 the first operational HUD unit was installed into the Blackburn Buccaneer. Initially HUDs were used for gun sighting/firing and a few basic

instruments, but the next generation of HUD systems, developed for the Hawker Siddeley Harrier, provided primary flight information, navigation data and a weapon aiming system. As well as the Harrier this HUD was also adopted by the RAF's Jaguar fleet.

Modern HUDs combine the projected image with the pilot's field of view to produce a composite 3D image, with computer-generated imagery and symbols displayed by the projection system. Data varies depending on whether the HUD is installed in a fighter jet or in a transport plane.

Head Up Display on a C-130J Hercules

94 Helmet Mounted Display

Taking the concept of the Head Up Display (HUD) and transporting it directly into the 21st Century is the Helmet Mounted Display System found in the Striker II helmet from BAE Systems. Worn by RAF Typhoon pilots it is one most advanced pieces of avionic equipment in the world and promises to revolutionise air-to-air combat.

The helmet is a sophisticated piece of kit that comprises a protective helmet, a helmet mounted sight (HMS), night vision, microphone, headphones with noise cancelling technology and an oxygen mask. Imagery projected onto the visor includes speed, heading, altitude and the exact position of any enemy missiles or aircraft. However, the real party-piece of the HMS is that it allows the pilot to 'see' through the plane they are flying. Using a data sensor in the nose of the aircraft when a pilot simply looks down to the position of the terrain underneath him (along any enemy aircraft) it is projected in high definition onto his visor. He can then 'lock on' to any target just by looking at it and by a simple voice command; he no longer needs to have his aircraft pointing in the right direction before he can fire his weapons, the Striker II does all the pointing. Wherever the pilot turns, so do the weapons and sensors.

Fully integrated weapons system. In a helmet.

The Striker II helmet incorporates full high definition displays with 3D audio. With an integrated night vision camera it also eliminates the need for heavy and cumbersome night vision goggles. A pilot can look at multiple targets, prioritise them via voice controls and and prime weapons just by moving his head.

DefenceImagery/OGLv1.0

The Striker II helmets are made to measure, with the pilot's head scanned using a laser to gather accurate measurements for both size and shape. It is reported that each helmet costs around **£288,000**

Moments of
Reflection and
Memory

95 1943: Colours and Memorials

1943 was a significant moment in the history of the RAF for a number of reasons. Firstly, it was the 25th anniversary of its institution and with that came the idea of Colours. However, because of wartime austerity it was not possible to present any.

The Queen's Colours are awarded by the Sovereign in recognition of service or achievement. Eight of them have been awarded to formations and establishments of the Royal Air Force and one to the Royal Auxiliary Air Force. A Colour measures 3ft 9in square and is affixed to a pike 8ft 2in in length, surmounted by a Royal Crown in gold.

On 27 December 1947, King George VI approved the award of Colours to the Royal Air Force, the Royal Air Force College Cranwell and No. 1 School of Technical Training. King George VI presented the first Colour to the Royal Air Force College Cranwell on 6 July 1948.

Queen's Colours are normally replaced every fifteen years.

1943 was also the year in which the RAF Ensign was added to the flags on the national war memorial (the Cenotaph) in London. The Cenotaph was unveiled on 11 November 1920 with a Union Jack, White Ensign and Red Ensign on one side, and a Union Jack, White Ensign and Blue Ensign on the other. After the RAF Ensign was instituted in 1921 it was occasionally suggested that it should be added to the flags on the Cenotaph. The idea was always rejected on the grounds that the ensign had not existed during the war and that the Royal Air Force had only been formed just a few months before the Armistice was signed.

In February 1943, Chief of the Air Staff, Air Marshall Sir Charles Portal, obtained an informal agreement from Buckingham Palace that the Royal Air Force should be represented on the Cenotaph by the addition of an RAF Ensign on each side of the monument. This was passed on to the Prime Minister, Winston Churchill, who replied that he did not want any changes. Eventually though, after obtaining the agreement from the First Lord of the Admiralty and the Secretary of State at the War Office, Churchill reluctantly agreed.

At the request of the Admiralty there was no official ceremony for the addition of the ensign. All the flags on the Cenotaph were changed immediately after dawn on 1 April 1943, an RAF Ensign replacing the White Ensign on the west side. At 11.30am a Royal Air Force Regiment guard paraded at the Cenotaph and a wreath was placed beneath the RAF Ensign.

Nine Colours

The first Colour to be presented, was to the RAF College, Cranwell, on 6 July 1948. It was replaced on 30 May 1975. Other Colours have been presented to the RAF as follows:

No. 1 School of Technical Training, RAF Halton: 25 July 1952

RAF Regiment: 17 March 1953, replaced 1967

Near East Air Force: 14 October 1960, laid up 31 May 1976

Far East Air Force: 13 July 1961, laid up 13 June 1972

Central Flying School: 26 June 1969

RAF Germany: 16 September 1970

Royal Auxiliary Air Force: presented 1989

The Queen's Colours for the RAF

96 The Air Forces Memorial

The Air Forces Memorial (also known as the Runnymeade Memorial was designed by Sir Edward Maufe and unveiled on 17 October 1953 by Queen Elizabeth II. The memorial commemorates 20,287 airmen and women who were lost during WW2 operations from bases in the United Kingdom and North and Western Europe who have no known grave.

Maurice Savage / Alamy

97 The Battle of Britain Memorial

The Battle of Britain Memorial was the brainchild of Wing Commander Geoffrey Page who flew Hurricanes with 56 Squadron, RAF during the Battle. The memorial is situated within "Hellfire Corner" an area of Kent over which much of the aerial combat took place and was opened by Her Majesty Queen Elizabeth the Queen Mother on 9th July 1993.

Marc Henry / Alamy

98 Bomber Command Memorial

Officially unveiled by Her Majesty The Queen on 28th June 2012, the Bomber Command Memorial is located in Green Park, London and commemorates the 55,573 members of Bomber Command who lost their lives in the Second World War.

Tim Rademacher/WikiCommons

99 Battle of Britain Memorial Flight

The Battle of Britain Memorial Flight (BBMF) is a living memorial to the aircrews of WW2, providing inspiring air displays at events across the UK. Operating and maintaining five different types of historic aircraft – Spitfire, Lancaster, Hurricane, Dakota, Chipmunk – they can be seen flying at events commemorating WW2, at high-profile British state events such as Trooping the Colour and the Queen's birthday, along with regular appearances at air shows across the UK.

In the years following WW2 it became traditional for a Spitfire and Hurricane to lead the Victory Day flypast over London. From there came the idea to pull together a historic collection of airworthy machines to commemorate the Battle of Britain and the wider accomplishments of the RAF during the war. In 1957 the Historic Aircraft Flight was formed at RAF Biggin Hill with one Hurricane (LF363) and three Mk XIX Spitfires (PM631, PS853 and PS915).

Over the years more aircraft have been purchased and in March 1976 the Flight moved to its current base at RAF Coningsby.

Spitfire, Lancaster and Hurricane of the BBMF

The BBMF operates five different historical aircraft:

- ● **Avro Lancaster**
- ● **Supermarine Spitfires**
- ● **Hawker Hurricanes**
- ● **Douglas Dakota**
- ● **de Havilland Canada DHC-1 Chipmunks**

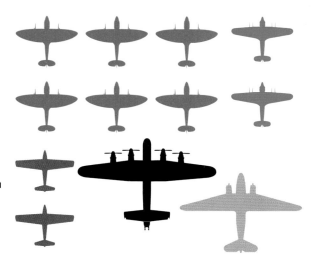

"There are few sights or sounds able to evoke more powerful thoughts and emotions than that of the Battle of Britain Memorial Flight flying overhead. To some it commemorates loved ones and relatives who fought and died in the air during the Second World War; to others it is an example of this nation's resilience and indomitable spirit in the face of adversity; for yet others it represents a tangible link between the modern RAF and its illustrious forefathers, and it continues to inspire in many young people a desire to serve this country in the air."

HM Queen Elizabeth II's tribute to the BBMF in 2007 on its 50th anniversary

Lancaster PA474

The BBMF's Lancaster bomber - PA474, was acquired by the BBMF in 1973 and is one of only two surviving airworthy examples of the type; the other is in Canada. She was built in mid-1945 and assigned to reconnaissance duties after appearing too late to take part in the bombing of Japan.

Typical formation

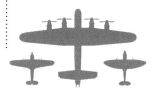

100 The RAF Benevolent Fund

The Royal Air Force Benevolent Fund (RAFBF) is the Royal Air Force's leading welfare charity, providing financial, practical and emotional support to serving and former members of the RAF – regardless of rank – as well as their partners and dependents.

Lord Trenchard set up the RAFBF in 1919 in an effort to offer support and assistance to those who had served in the RAF during the WW1 and their families. The fledgling RAF had endured 16,000 casualties, leaving 2,600 widows and dependents and 7,500 badly incapacitated men, who often had little or no chance of employment for the rest of their lives. Back then some examples of the kind of help they could offer included giving a shilling for a night's lodging so the recipient had a chance to seek work or to provide tools or repair boots.

In 1919 the RAFB spent

£919

In 2016 the figure was more than

£17m

That money helps around

41,000

serving RAF Personnel, veterans and their dependents.

Memorials as well as veterans

As well as helping individuals, the RAFBF is also responsible looking after both the Bomber Command Memorial in Green Park, London and the RAF Memorial which is situated on the Victoria Embankment, also in central London.

Donate to the RAFBF

The Royal Air Force Benevolent Fund receives no public funding and relies on donations from the public to carry out its support. If you would like to help, you can donate directly at www.rafbf.org